C000185810

Crochet for Beginners Handbook

2 Manuscripts In 1 Book For A Complete Crochet Beginners Guide With Illustrations, Step-By-Step Instructions and over 50 Crochet Patterns Included

Nancy Gordon

Crochet for Beginners

A Complete Step By Step Guide with Picture illustrations to Learn Crocheting the Quick & Easy Way

Nancy Gordon

Contents

Book 2
Easy Crochet Patterns for Beginners

Additionally, the information in the following pages is intended only for informational purposes and should thus be thought of as universal. As befitting its nature, it is presented without assurance regarding its prolonged validity or interim quality. Trademarks that are mentioned are done without written consent and can in no way be considered an endorsement from the trademark holder.

Introduction

Crocheting is an old favorite pastime, pretty much like stamp collecting, and coin collecting. These hobbies were incredibly popular back in the day when electronic gadgets didn't get in the way of our leisure time. Often times, when we imagine crochet, we think of our grandmothers crocheting a table runner or placemats in her rocking chair. At a certain time, it seemed as though the world had lost its interest in arts and craft. However, with blogs and social media accounts that focus on craft, such as *Diply*, *Pinterest*, *Buzzfeed* and *Tastemade*, crocheting and other long-forgotten handicrafts are making a comeback, albeit with a fresher twist compared to what our grandmothers used to do. Crocheting as we see it today was not how it was done back then.

A quick search on *Instagram* will show you plenty of ways to make cool crop tops, comfortable shoes, bags, phone covers, dream catchers, as well as cute dolls. Thanks to its new techniques and tools, crocheting has turned into a trendy and modern craft.

So, if you've ever looked at a crocheting video and thought, *I want to do that too*, then you're in luck! Because in this book, we will teach you the fundamentals of crocheting, starting from the how-to's, know-hows, techniques, and patterns.

If you are new to the art of crocheting, going through the number of hooks, stitches, yarns, and patterns may all seem confusing and even overwhelming at first, but this book will take you on a journey that will uncover all the basics, so you don't feel overwhelmed.

In this book, we will learn a little bit about the history of crocheting as well as the supplies that you will need. We will also discuss basic crochet patterns, and how to crochet effectively. This book aims to help you firmly grasp the basics of crochet whether it's selecting the right supplies, what hook size conversions are required as beginners, standard yarn weights and figuring out what specialist abbreviations and symbols are. At the very end, we will also investigate how to complete a variety of basic crochet stitches!

Chapter 1:
How to Read and Understand Crochet

To pick up or start any kind of new craft or hobby, one must first get acquainted with the language of that particular art. It's the same case with crocheting – before attempting to read crochet patterns, you must first develop an understanding of the craft. This is fairly similar to looking up recipes. When we first set eyes on a recipe, we scan the list of ingredients, the cooking time, as well as instructions to see if it is something that we can attempt based on our prior skill level. It is the same with crochet patterns. To give you an idea, here are a couple of factors you should keep in mind before you sit down to crochet:

1- Level of Difficulty

The level of difficulty is one of the first aspects to consider. Almost all crochet patterns are rated either *beginner*, *easy*, *intermediate*, or *experienced*. Beginner patterns are, of course, suitable for those who are new to crocheting as it requires basic stitches that are simple to create simple. If you're a beginner, start with easier stitches and work your way up. Once you've learned the ropes, you can move up to more advanced patterns.

2- Check the Gauge

Checking the gauge on your patterns ensures that your outcome is the right size. After this, you would also need to count your stitches as you go along so you can keep track of how many stitches there are in each row.

3- Practice

Like every form of art or skill, excelling at crocheting requires patience, perseverance, and practice. You will struggle at first – this is precisely why you must start with beginner patterns to grasp the basics. But as you continue crocheting more and more, you will eventually get the hang of it, and will be to attempt more advanced patterns in no time.

Crochet Terms and Abbreviations

Crochet patterns use specific codes, and no, they aren't used to confuse you! These codes help along the process, allowing users to understand patterns much better and faster.

Practicing beginner crochet patterns will help you memorize each code until it eventually becomes second nature to you. Here is a list of common abbreviations that you will find while crocheting patterns. These codes enable users to better understand things and make pattern books easier to follow. Keep this list handy for when you are crocheting and if you come across a term that's not on this list, inspect your pattern chart for more insight and add it to this list:

Abbreviation	Meaning
Approx.	Approximately
Beg	Begin(ning)
Bet	Between
Blp	Back Loop Only
Bp	Back Post
Cc	Contrast Color
Ch	**Chain Stitch**
Dc	**Double Crochet**
Dec	Decrease(S)(D)(Ing)
Dtr	Double Treble Crochet
Flp	Front Loop Only
Foll	Follow(Ing)
Fp	Front Post
Hdc	**Half Double Crochet**
Inc	Increase(S)(D)(Ing)
Mc	Main Color
Pat	Pattern
Rem	Remaining
Rep	Repeat
Rib	Ribbing
Rs	Right Side
Sc	**Single Crochet**
Sl St	**Slip Stitch**
St(S)	Stitch(Es)
Tog	Together
Tr	**Treble Crochet**
Ws	Wrong Side
Yo	**Yarn Over Hook**

How to Read Crochet Pattern Instructions

Once you've familiarized yourself with these abbreviations, your next task is to understand the symbols included in the world of crocheting. These symbols or special characters represent clarifications, as well as repetitions in patterns or specific directions. Understanding them is vital to create patterns and develop your skills.

Symbol	Meaning
( )	This symbol is known as *parentheses*. It is used to signify repetitiveness in an action or a stitch. If you come across this sign, you are meant to repeat a stitch in succession. This symbol is typically followed by a number indicating the number of stitches you have to make. This pattern can also be used to signify a group of directions, all using the same specific stitch.
[ ]	These square brackets indicate that you must repeat a stitch pattern. This is required when working in correspondence with a parenthesis. On the other hand, it can also be used to clarify information.
{ }	This symbol is used to indicate repetitive instructions, often ones worked within another set of bracketed directions.
* • ♦ †	Asterisks, bullet points, diamonds, plus signs, and other special characters indicate that the person crocheting must repeat the series of stitches.

To help you understand the symbols mentioned above and how to follow them, here are some working examples:

Example 1:

Row 1: With size H hook, ch 15, sc in 2nd ch from hook and in each ch across, turn. (14 sc)

1. Here, you need to stitch the first row using a size H crochet hook.

2. Make 15 chain stitches.

3. Create a single crochet in the second chain stitch from the hook.

4. Create each chain stitch across, then turn the piece.

   (A repetition of 14 single crochet stitches is required in the first row.)

Example 2:

Row 2: ch 1, 2 sc in first sc, sc in each rem sc across to last sc, 2 sc in last sc, turn. (16 sc)

1. Begin the second row with a chain stitch.

2. Make two single crochets in the previous row's single crochet stitch.

3. Make single crochet stitch in every single crochet on the first row till you reach the final one.

4. Last single crochet in that row, make two single crochets then turn the piece

(There are 16 single crochet stitches in the first row).

Example 3:

(dc in next sc, ch 2, skip next two sc) twice

1. Parentheses indicate that you must repeat the instructions according to the number of times mentioned.

2. Create a double crochet stitch in the next single crochet.

3. Next, make two chain stitches.

4. Then skip the next two single crochets from the previous row.

5. All of above mentioned steps need to be repeated.

Once completed twice, you can then move on to the next set of instructions.

Rounds and Rows

The examples mentioned above are stitches that require you to work in rows, meaning you simply have to continue stitching straight across. There will be times when you would need to work in rounds or in a circle. When working with rows, simply turn your piece each time you reach the end of the row. This will create a turning chain, then you can continue working again across the top of that specific row and create another new row. When you work in rounds, you are stitching in a spiral which means you are not required to turn your piece around - you only need to continue rotating. 'RND' is usually the abbreviation for round stitches which is usually shown at the start of each direction. When you see 'Row', this means you need to be crocheting in a row.

How to Read Crochet Pattern Symbols and Charts

With written instructions, you are likely to find a crochet design in the form of a chart containing more symbols. The symbols are a lot easier to understand and read. Since this book is for beginners, the symbols have been simplified as shown above. This will only show you basic crochet stitches that you'll need to know as a beginner.

Don't worry about not understanding the symbols and abbreviations described here. This information is for you to know and, while it is important, most people who crochet prefer referring to charts.

Single crochets, chain stitches, slip stitches, as well as half double crochets, double crochets, and treble crochets, are all stitches that will make up at least 90% of your stitching repertoire and each of these will be indicated clearly.

The starting point of any design is typically indicated using a black triangle Δ or similar, and it is usually accompanied by a row of chain stitches.

Chapter 2:
Crocheting Supplies

With any craft, you will always need the appropriate tools to get the job done right. No proper tools, no work of art. In this chapter, we will look at the necessary tools needed to craft any kind of crocheting pattern, whether you are working with a beginner, intermediate, or advanced pattern.

To craft successfully, you will need:

A Crochet Hook

A crochet hook is practically the most important tool of all. Having no hook is like having no camera to take pictures. This tool allows you to create loops in the yarn and interlock these loops into stitches. The crochet hook has a pointy hook end to make it easier for you to insert yarns and hook them. It also has a slanted groove underneath that enables folks to pull loops through easily.

These hooks are made using a variety of materials with the most common being aluminum, wood, and plastic. They also come in various sizes depending on the kind of yarn you're using. For beginners, it is recommended you start crocheting using a basic aluminum crochet hook that is mid-range in size. This allows the beginner to acquire greater control when stitching and looping.

Yarn

The second most important item on the list is yarn. Without it, one can obviously not crochet. The composition of the yarn can vary depending on the crochet project. Yarn is typically made from spun organic fibers that are derived from alpaca and wool. Both these materials are great in providing warmth and elasticity.

Synthetic fibers such as acrylics are also used as an alternative. For beginners, you want to use yarn that is easy to work with, so go for yarn that comes in light, solid colors rather than those with multi-colored strands. This is crucial because it will help you distinguish your stitches as you go about learning different types of stiches.

As a beginner, you also want to use worsted weight yarn. This is a type of medium-weight yarn that is very versatile and extremely easy to work with. This yarn is perfect for creating large blankets and small Japanese amigurumi toys.

Scissors

Almost all craft projects require scissors. You will require it to snip yarn or loose threads for stitching purposes. There are no special scissors for crocheting, but you do want to get a pair of reliable quality scissors. It is advisable you get a pair with a sharp pointed end. Make sure the pointed end is small enough to make quick, clean, and precise cuts. Dressmaking scissors are not recommended as they make it harder to cut with precision.

Crochet Hook Size Conversion Chart

You should be aware of all the different kinds of hooks available for crocheting. This will help you in selecting the correct yarn type. Most hooks already have their metric millimeters stamped on them, so it makes figuring out the hook sizes much easier. The hook size must correspond with the thickness of the yarn. The thicker the yarn, the thicker hook diameter you will need. As for thinner yarns, you can work with thinner hooks of course.

Here is a simple conversion chart for you to compare the metric measurements between UK and US crochet hook sizes. This will make it easier for you to select a yarn according to the diameter. Keep in mind that hook sizes may vary depending on the manufacturer, hence this chart is a simple guide for you to get started.

Metric (millimeters)	UK Size	US Size
2 mm	14	-
2.25 mm	13	B-1
2.5 mm	12	-
2.75 mm	-	C-2
3 mm	11	-
3.25 mm	10	D-3
3.5 mm	9	E-4
3.75 mm	-	F-5
4 mm	8	G-6
4.5 mm	7	7
5 mm	6	H-8
5.5 mm	5	I-9
6 mm	4	J-10
6.5 mm	3	K-10.5
7 mm	2	-
7 mm	2	-
9 mm	00	M/N-13
10 mm	000	N/P-15

Standard Crochet Yarn Weights Chart

Names associated with crochet yarns may also vary in the UK and the US, just like the crochet hooks. It also varies according to the manufacturer. Moving further, beginners find is the usage of 'yarn weight,' which does not mean the weight of the ball of yarn but rather the thickness of the thread. Of course, once you know, it is relatively easy.

In crocheting, the thicker the yarn, the heavier the weight. Once you get acquainted with this idea, it will be easy to understand why it is done this way. The yarn is categorized according to specific weights to make it easier for beginners to know what crochet hook to use and how big the stitches need to be.

US Yarn Weight Name	UK Yarn Weight Name	Gauge Range ('sts' - stitches) per 4 inches	Crochet Hook Range (millimeters)
0 / Lace	2-ply	32 - 42 sts	1.5 mm - 2.25 mm
1 / Super Fine	3-ply / Sport / Baby	21 - 32 sts	2.25 mm - 3.5 mm
2 / Fine	4-ply / Baby	16 - 20 sts	3.5 mm - 4.5 mm
3 / Light	DK / Light Worsted	12 - 17 sts	4.5 mm - 5.5 mm
4 / Medium	Aran / Worsted	11 - 14 sts	5. 5 mm - 6.5 mm
5 / Bulky	Chunky / Rug	8 - 11 sts	6.5 mm – 9mm
6 / Super Bulky	Super Chunky	7 - 9 sts	9 mm – 15 mm

US & UK Yarn Weight Names

To fully comprehend the table shown above, here is a description of each column:

US Yarn Weight Name & UK Yarn Weight Name

These two titles refer to the yarn weight in each country. In the US, measurements are relatively simple to understand with numbers that indicate thickness, but in the UK, the term 'ply' often follows the weights mentioned.

Ply is just another term for 'strand,' so the number you see beforehand is the number of strands that need to be twisted together to create a thread of yarn. For instance, a 2-ply yarn would require two strands to create the yarn, while a 4-ply yarn would need a total of four strands. The higher the ply, the stronger it is, with more density, durability, and elasticity.

Gauge Range & Crochet Hook Range

In this column, the number indicates how many stitches a person is required to make for every four inches of crochet piece. This is a wide estimation. Each crochet person has their own way of performing stitches depending on the level of tightness. The chart suggests the range of stitches that the yarn weight can stitch up to. When looking at that column, you must also learn what *gauge* means.

In crocheting, gauge refers to the tension needed to produce a piece in the correct size. Simply stated, the higher the hook size, the smaller the gauge range and higher the weight of the yarn would be. For instance, if you are crocheting using chunky yarn, you would only need between eight to eleven stitches every four inches. You will also need a bigger crochet hook to handle the weight of the yarn.

The table given here is a rough guide that will help you select the right hook according to the gauge for your pattern. It is extremely crucial to work with the correct gauge, especially when you are creating clothing, or else the finished product may not fit well or turn out to be the appropriate size. Most yarn manufacturers make our lives easier by listing both the 'stitches' and 'rows' under their gauge information on yarn labels. This suggests the number of stitches the yarn will be able to complete in a four by four section, and it also tells you how many rows the yarn will be able to make.

Most patterns also provide this information. For instance, you would see a pattern with *16 sts and 14 rows in a 4" square.* The best way to go about this is to make a 4-inch swatch sample and practice your gauge on the stitch pattern before you begin your project. To accomplish this, first look at the yarn weight, followed by the hook size, then the stitch pattern, and finally the gauge information. When you use the correct materials, test it out by completing a 4-inch swatch using the number of stitches specified in the pattern, both across as well as rows down. Next, count the number of stitches and rows in your sample. If you have completed too many rows and stitches, this means you have worked too tightly. To rectify this, a bigger hook may be used to manage the quantity of stitches.

As always, practicing your crocheting is key until you are able to achieve the correct gauge for your patterns.

Chapter 3:
Types of Crochet

When we talk about yarn, plenty of people assume yarn is only meant for knitting. Not to mention, many people think knitting and crocheting are the same. Knitting and crocheting have a number of distinctions, especially when it comes to the tools needed to crochet.

Crocheting has its very own finishes, tools, and techniques, and none of this can be achieved through knitting. In Europe, crocheting began to grow in the early nineteenth century, and at that point, it was known as 'shepherd's knitting.' People found this name befitting because crochet seemed like a cheap alternative to purchasing expensive cloth and lace. With the rule of Queen Victoria, crocheting was made popular thanks to her as she was found purchasing Irish lace crochet items from the people of Ireland during the potato famine. Queen Victoria also picked up crocheting herself which popularized the craft throughout England.

Crochet is not only historic in this sense, but it was also a lifesaver. Many poor families were pulled out of starvation because of the potato famine by crocheting. They used their skills to create items which eventually helped them earn enough to migrate to America. In the 1900s, Irish folks landed in the US bringing with them their crocheting skills. During the war in the 1950s, crocheting was used for making items such as under-helmet caps and nets for soldiers. It was also used by women to embellish dresses and hats, particularly when they did not have access to money and resources. During the 1960s, it was all the rage for women to have crochet fabric and they began crocheting their own pantsuits and shift dresses.

The rise of crocheting rose in popularity in the 1970s as granny squares made their debut in dresses, jackets, and hooded sweatshirts that were made entirely out of these motifs. Next came the 1980s, and there was a full-blown rise in crochet-use in fashion from crochet cardigans, to fete style toys. Sometime in the 1990s, crocheting dwindled, but as explained earlier in the book, with the internet and Instagram and other social media platforms, crocheting is back with a modern makeover for all things stylish, from kid's toys to home accessories, to clothing items for both women and men. As beginners, it is also good to know the different types of crochet that exists in our world. Take note that crocheting was not a thing in Europe or America. Different variations existed in different parts of the world to be used for a variety of uses from bags to traditional headgear, clothing, bracelets, adornments, as well as home decor.

Here is a list of 21 well-known crocheting types that still exist in the world and are being practiced everywhere:

1. Amigurumi Crochet

This is the most popular form of crochet, and its country of origin is Japan. Amigurumi refers to the art of creating small, stuffed toys or objects from crocheted yarn. Ami means to crochet or even to knit, whereas nuigurumi refers to stuffed dolls. Whenever you see a doll or toy made of yarn, it is most likely amigurumi. Many popular culture items have been used to make amigurumi such as Hello Kitty, Mario Brothers, Pokemon, and Winnie the Pooh.

Items made using Amigurumi crochet:

- Children's toys

2. Aran Crochet

This type of crochet is usually cabled or ribbed. It has its roots in Celtic culture and features interlocking cables. It is often the choice of crochet used for making bigger items such as scarves, sweaters, and beanies. If you see the word 'Aran' in your patterns, be careful because Aran is also used to describe the weight of yarn. Cozy blankets and throws are usually made using Aran crochet.

Items made using Aran crochet:

- Blankets
- Jackets
- Coats
- Scarves
- Throws

3. Bavarian Crochet

This Bavarian type of crochet is a vintage crochet stitch, and it is traditionally used in rounds. The resulting piece is often a thick fabric that procures for smooth and blended color changes compared to sharp color changes such as the ones commonly seen in a granny square. With Bavarian crochet, you will work in two parts. The first part is the base of clusters whereas the second part is followed by a row of shells. The Bavarian crochet is the fancier cousin to the granny square.

Items made using Bavarian crochet:

- Blankets
- Shawls
- Tabletop covers

4. Bosnian Crochet

This type of crochet has a knit-like fabric and is quite dense in nature. It is crocheted using a slip stitch and crocheted in different parts from the row before. Bosnian crochet also uses a different type of hook, conveniently called Bosnian crochet hook which you can buy, but using regular hooks can work just as well. This type of crochet is called Shepherd's knitting since it also looks like knitted fabrics.

Items made using Bosnian crochet:

- Scarves
- Beanies
- Socks
- Hand gloves

5. Bullion Crochet

This crochet is a specialized stitch and is achieved using a combination of multiple yarn wraps on a long crochet hook. The result is a distinctive roll stitch which appears quite unique too. Motifs are usually made using bullion crochet, and it results in a uniform, thick, and round motif style piece.

Items made using Bullion crochet:
- Stiff items such as placemats
- Motifs for decoration

6. Broomstick Crochet

Also known as jiffy lace, broomstick crochet is a type of vintage crochet stitch, which is made with a traditional crochet hook. The resulting stitches are formed around a long and wide object such as broomstick handle, which is how it gets its name. Modern people who crochet use larger crochet hooks or even thick dowels when doing a broomstick crochet. This type of crochet is an excellent skill to learn and master as its final product is very beautiful and unique.

Items made using Broomstick crochet:

- Delicate shawls
- Throw blankets for decoration

7. Bruges Crochet

Ribbons of crochet can be created using bruges crochet. These ribbons are then crocheted together, and the results show an intricate lace pattern. This is also the most common type of crochet used in home decor items.

Items made using Bruges crochet:

- Intricate shawls
- Embellishments for clothing

- Table mats

8. Clothesline Crochet

In this crochet style, traditional crochet stitches are done over a clothesline or thick rope or even thick twine to make baskets, and circular mats to hold their shape. This type of crocheting can be traced back to Africa and Nepal.

Items made using clothesline crochet:

- Baskets
- Mats
- Structural wall hangings

9. Clones Lace Crochet

This type of crochet is associated with the Irish lace crochet. It was created to be an alternative to the Irish lace crochet because it's easier and quicker to make than the Irish needlepoint lace. The clones knot used for this type of crocheting requires a unique crochet skillset. Clones lace is a very practical crochet style, and it was commonly used during wars since it was quick and fast to make.

Items made using clones lace crochet:

- Open weave scarves
- Delicate dresses and tops

10. Cro-hook Crochet

This uniquely named crochet is created using a double-ended hook to create double-sided crochet. This enables you to make stitches on or off at either end of the crochet piece, and this piece does not have a wrong or right side to work on. Because of its nature, this type of crochet is called the Cro-hook or the Cro-knit. This type of crochet closely resembles the Tunisian crochet and is an excellent option if you're working with colors that aren't manageable with other types of crochet.

Items made using clones lace crochet:

- Washcloths
- Scarves
- Baby blankets

11. Filet Crochet

This style is created using chain rows and double crochet stitches. What you get is a grid-like pattern wherein the squares are either filled or not filled, and the negative space is usually there to create images with the pieces. The wonderful thing about this type of crochet is that you can go full-on creative and embed images using empty or full squares of fabric.

Items made using filet crochet:

- Baby blankets
- Jackets and kimonos
- Handbags
- Cushions

12. Finger Crochet

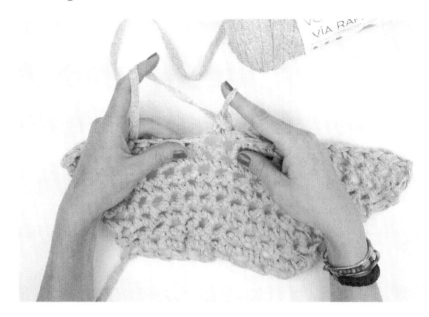

This type of crochet is called as such because it does not require hooks. It is similar to finger knitting. It's basically hand fabric which you can use to weave crochet stitches. This is a fun crochet to do when you are a beginner, but the resulting piece has loose tension which is probably why people move on to hooks to make more versatile projects.

Items made using finger crochet:

- Simple string bags
- Basic scarves

13. Freeform Crochet

This type of crochet is called freeform because there is no pattern or plan to follow. It is entirely up to the person crocheting to create something. This type of crochet is very artistic and organic, making it an excellent option for beginners. However, if you find yourself struggling without instructions or even a plan, then it's best to avoid freeform and follow crochet pieces with patterns.

Items made using freeform crochet:

- One-off clothing items
- Art pieces

14. Hairpin Crochet

Like the broomstick crochet, the hairpin crochet is made using the traditional crochet hook, but instead of a broomstick, the piece is held taut using thin metal rods. In earlier times, this technique used actual hairpins which is how it got its name. The resulting piece is unique and beautiful.

Items made using hairpin crochet:

- Delicate scarves
- Shawls
- Wraps

15. Micro Crochet

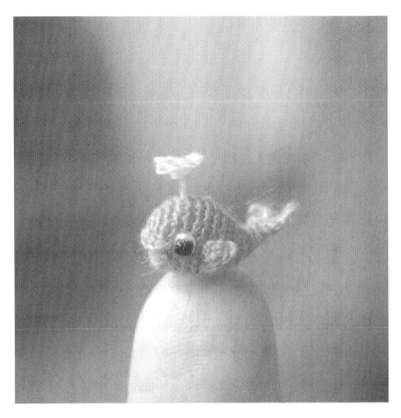

The micro crochet is a modern crochet style and is made using very fine yarn thread with extremely fine or small crochet hooks. It is a very delicate crocheting process and is great for those who are patient and like dainty and small things.

Item made using micro crochet:

- Tiny things for dollhouses
- Embellishments
- Talisman

16. Overlay Crochet

This technique is also quite unique where a base of crochet stitches is made, and then other stitches are added to the top to create a raised pattern. This crocheting technique is more advanced, and it brings many possibilities for you to create intricate pieces.

Items made using overlay crochet:

- Potholders
- Wall hangings
- Handbags

17. Pineapple Crochet

The pineapple crochet is considered more of a general stitch and shape rather than a technique. You can use this crochet to create scarves, doilies, and certain types of clothing. This stitch was very popular in the 1970s, and once you know how to spot this type of stitch, you will be seeing it everywhere.

Items made using pineapple crochet:

- Dresses
- Tops
- Shawls
- Wraps

18. Stained Glass Crochet

The stained glass crochet could be mistaken for the overlay crochet. However, it is different because the top part is normally made using only black yarn to accentuate the colors and create the stained glass effect. What you get is a very striking crochet pattern.

Items made using stained glass crochet:
- Thick, sturdy items
- Winter scarves
- Handbags

19. Symbol crochet

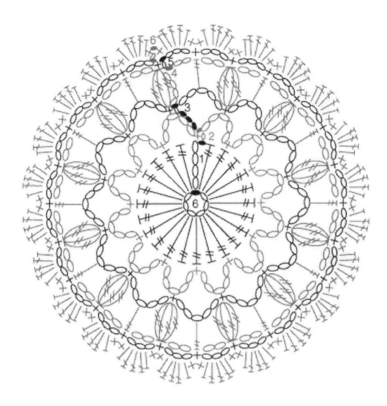

The symbol crochet is another type of popular crochet and is a favorite among the Japanese. It is also known as the "chart" crochet and is another one of those crochet skills that are crucial to learn because you can make any projects from any crochet books in any language and create them all by looking at a chart.

Items made using symbol crochet:

- Complicated patterns that are difficult to explain in words
- Intricate designs
- Motifs
- Foreign language patterns

20. Tapestry Crochet

As the name goes, plenty of color goes into creating this piece, and it is also known as "intarsia" crochet. Tapestry crochet is used in many different parts of the world, and it also has many different methods which result in a variety of styles. If you want to do color work, using tapestry crochet enables you to create intricate patterns with a variety of colored yarn.

Items made using tapestry crochet:

- Color workpieces
- Imagery based designs

21. Tunisian Crochet

This type of crochet is done on a long hook that has a stopper at the end. When you look at Tunisian crochet, it can be very similar to knitting because of the many live loops, and you need to work your loops on and off your hook, similar to knitting.

Items made using tapestry crochet:

- Knit-look items
- Blankets
- Scarves

Chapter 4:
How to Crochet for Right-Handers

Before we look at patterns, we need to study the fundamentals of crocheting which starts with how to hold a yarn. In this chapter, we will teach you not only how to crochet according to patterns, but also how to hold yarn, how to make knots and so on.

How to Hold the Yarn

One of the first things you must learn is how to hold your yarn properly. This comes before learning to secure the yarn on the crochet hook. Holding the yarn may differ depending on whether you are a right-hander or left-hander. If you are a right-hander, your left hand will be your yarn hand, and your right hand will be the one that holds the crochet hook.

To begin, use your left hand and bring the yarn between your little finger and ring finger and wrap it just once, making a loop around the bottom little finger.

Next, move the yarn across diagonally on the inside of your hand. Then, make another loop on your ring finger by bringing it to the top of the index finger and looping it to the inside of the finger.

Next, create a slip knot. A slip knot is used to keep the yarn in place. This will give you greater control while stitching.

Firstly, lay your yarn down flat on the table. Take about six inches from the end of the yarn and create a loop that looks like a pretzel.

Next, hold the loop with your left hand and then move your crochet hook through the center of it, as seen in the image.

Next, tighten the loop around the hook by gently pulling both ends of the yarn. Allow a little allowance. Here, your slip knot should easily slide up and down the shaft of your hook, but it should be firm enough not come off over the end.

Using your middle finger and thumb to keep the yarn in place, clasp the yarn with your fingers and hold the crochet hook in your other hand. Holding your hook and yarn in this manner provides plenty of room for you to maneuver, and it also helps you control the yarn's tension by either lowering or raising your index finger.

Yarn Over

(Yo) or *yarn over* is one of the most common instructions that you will find in your crochet patterns because it is a very crucial pattern and element for each stitch. Yarn over requires you to simply loop the yarn over your hook. This process is incredibly simple. Once you are done with your slip knot, take the longer length of your yarn behind the hook and bring it over the top of the hook, then move it right into the throat to hook the yarn from the bottom.

Chain Stitch

Chain stitch or (ch) is another crucial stitch in crocheting, and it makes its appearance in just about any crochet pattern. This type of stitch is usually found at the beginning of each crochet project because it allows you to build a foundation of chain stitches which you can then build upon. The chain stitch is also known as a *joining stitch* which serves two purposes: beginning your project, and structurally connecting the previous row with the new one.

Creating the chain stitch also begins after you are done doing the slip knot. Next, hold your yarn and hook following the image above. You need to hold the tail of the slip knot between your thumb and middle finger at the same time.

Next, yarn over and then rotate the hook so that the hook faces downwards toward the slip knot.

Once done, gently tug the hook while holding the wrapped yarn, through the loop on the slip knot, and rotate the hook back upwards as you come out to the other side. This forms a chain stitch. Take note not to make the loop too tight. Don't worry if this sounds confusing. You will get the hang of it after one or two tries.

You can continue the chain stitch by repeating this process by pulling the yarn through the second loop. You need to ensure that your chain stitches are the same size so that an even tension can be procured. Once you are done completing the stitches recommended by your pattern, you have yourself a foundation chain.

How to Make a 'Magic Ring' also known as the Adjustable Loop

The stitches described above are mainly for straight patterns. It teaches you how to begin your stitching in rows. Moving forward, we will investigate designing in rounds. To begin a circular crochet pattern, learning how to make an adjustable loop is one of the easiest ways to get started. It also provides a neater finish compared to slip knots and chain stitches.

First, begin by wrapping the yarn twice around your index finger, then carefully insert the crochet hook underneath the yarn making sure to hook the second loop.

Next, pull the yarn back through the way it was inserted to create a loop.

Just like straight patterns, round patterns also require foundation chains, and this is dependent on the number of chain stitches your pattern calls for.

Create your chain stitches the way it is described above. Continue working around the loop according to the instructions on your pattern until you are done with your first round.

Gently tug at the yarn's tail to tighten the center ring so that the stitches close elegantly together.

Single Crochet Stitch

The single crochet stitch is another regular crochet stitch and is usually signified with the abbreviation (sc). This stitch is flat and tight, and it forms a compacted, finished piece, more so than other stitches. It is an extremely popular stitch used in amigurumi.

Another commonly used stitch found in crochet is the single crochet (sc) stitch. It's quite popular because of its tight and flat nature, it forms a denser finished piece compared to other stitches. Thus, it is especially popular in amigurumi!

One of the first things to do is to create a foundation chain using chain stitches. The number of stitches you need to make corresponds to the number of single crochet stitches you want your row to have including one additional chain stitch.

The first row of chain stitch that you make is called your *turning chain*. This means you will be using it to form a new row. Because of this, you can skip this stitch and insert your hook into the second chain stitch from the hook which would give you two loops of yarn around your crochet hook.

Next, yarn over and then rotate your hook's throat towards yourself and then pull it through the first loop, taking the wrapped yarn with you. You will end up with two loops around your hook.

Next, yarn over again and then pull it through both loops. By now, you should only have one loop around your hook. You have now completed a single crochet stitch!

To complete a whole row of single crochet, repeat three and four in the chain stitch until you have reached the end of your row.

How to Make a Turning Chain

Firstly, congratulations on creating your first row of stitches. Now it is time to take your basic stitches to the next level. Once you are done with the first row, you will need a turning chain to add height which allows you to crochet back on your own and complete another new row. These turning chains are a combination of chain stitches, and the number of chain stitches you need to create depends on what your follow-up stitch is going to be. Follow this simple guideline:

Name of Stitch	Number of Chain Stitches
Slip Stitch (sl st)	0
Single Crochet (sc)	1
Half Double Crochet (hdc)	2
Double Crochet (dc)	3
Treble Crochet (tr)	4
Double Treble Crochet (dtr)	5

Create chain stitches in the chain stitch at the end of your first row of stitches. This will result in a turning chain.

Next, flip your crochet over so that the hook stays on the right side instead of being on the left side.

When you begin your next row, insert your crochet hook into the space next to the bottom of your turning chain. The bottom is basically the first stitch of the row. Continue stitching using the stitch that your pattern requires. Next, when you have completed another row, continue repeating the steps according to the number of rows required.

Slip Stitch

Also known as (sl st) the *slip stitch* is the flattest type of crochet stitch there is in crocheting and is chiefly used as a utility stitch to combine stitches that are used in round patterns. The best practice concerning this stitch is on the end of a foundation chain which allows you to create a ring.

As always, begin by creating a foundation chain of six stitches and then insert the hook into your first chain stitch which forms a ring.

Next, yarn over and then rotate the hook's throat facing yourself. This positions the crochet hook and yarn perfectly so that you can form the slip stitch.

Next, swiftly draw the wrapped yarn back through the chain stitch and through the loop that is already on your hook. This is your first stitch slip. What you should have now is one loop left on your hook.

Half Double Crochet Stitch

(hdc) is the abbreviation for *half double crochet* and this is a relatively weird (or more complicated) stitch. It can be categorized between a single crochet and a double crochet stitch height-wise. This stitch creates a relatively tight finished result similar to a single crochet, except this stitch provides a little more give like the double crochet does.

To start off, make your foundation stitch with chain stitches amounting to seventeen. The last two stitches are reserved for your turning chain.

Next, yarn over and insert the hook into the third chain stitch from the hook as shown in the image.

Yarn over, then gently tug at the yarn-wrapped hook
back through the chain stitch. You should now have
three loops around your hook.

Next, yarn over again and then pull the yarn through the three loops towards your crochet hook. You have now completed your first half double crochet stitch.

To continue creating an entire row of half double crochets, all you need to do is create a half double crochet stitches each in chain stitch on your foundation row right after you have completed the first one.

Double Crochet Stitch

(dc) is the abbreviation for this type of stitch and it is another common stitch used in crochet. It measures roughly twice the height of a single crochet stitch. The resulting pattern is often solid but not too stiff and is usually used to create shawls, afghans, home accessories as well as jumpers.

Ensure your foundation chain consists of eighteen stitches, leaving the three last stitches as your turning chain.

Do a yarn over and then insert your hook into the fourth chain stitch.

Yarn over and then pull it back gently through the chain stitch and take the wrapped yarn with you. You will now have three loops on your hook.

Next, yarn over and then pull the yarn through the first two loops - this will now create your double crochet stitch. You will now only have two loops around your hook.

Yarn over again and then gently pull the wrapped yarn again through the remaining two loops. This will result in completing your first ever double crochet stitch. You will only have one loop left on your crochet hook.

To complete an entire row of double crochet, you can start by making a double crochet stitch in every chain stitch on your foundation row.

Treble Crochet Stitch

(tr) is the abbreviation for *treble crochet* or *triple crochet* and it results in loose stitches that are slightly taller than the double crochet stitches. It is ideal for larger garments as well as home accessories.

Start by creating a nineteen-chain stitch foundation stitch, leaving the last four stitches for your turning chain.

Do a yarn over two times and then include your crochet hook directly into the fifth chain stitch from the hook.

Yarn over again and then gently pull the wrapped crochet hook back through the chain stitch. You now have all four loops on your hook.

Yarn over and then tug the yarn back through the first two loops on your hook.

Yarn over again and then pull the yarn back through the consecutively two loops on your hook.

Yarn over again and then pull the yarn back through the last two loops on your hook. Now you have completed your first treble crochet stitch with only one loop left on your crochet hook.

To complete the entire row of treble crochet, you need to yarn over twice and then insert your crochet hook into the next chain along your foundation chain.

Continue to create treble crochet stitches in each available chain stitch across the foundation chain until you have a complete row.

How to Fasten Off Your Yarn

Learning to fasten the end of your project is essential in any form of needlecraft. Just like in crocheting, you would also need to fasten your yarn at the end of your crochet piece so that it stays secure and in place, preventing your stitches from unraveling.

Cut your yarn and leave at least six inches of yarn from the hook. Next, pull the loose end through the final remaining loop on your hook. Remove the hook and tug gently on the yarn's tail to tighten the tail end.

Take a yarn needle and weave the yarn tail through two, three, or even four crochet stitches in your pattern to hide it.

Now you have yourself a final product with a perfectly neat finish!

Chapter 5:
How to Crochet for Left-Handers

Don't worry, we've got left-handed crocheters covered in this book too. Back in the day, left-handed crocheters had to learn the craft 'backwards' because they learned the craft from right-handed crocheters. But now, there is no need to do that any longer. There are plenty of tutorials, teachers and patterns for left-handed crocheters.

Basic Understanding of Left-Handed Crochet

Left-handed crochet is practically a mirror image of right-handed crochet. For left-handed crocheters, you would need to hold the crochet hook in your left hand and the yarn in the right hand. You can either use a knife grip or a pencil grip to hold the hook and manipulate the yarn the way a right-handed crocheter would do. While you can follow the instructions from your teacher or from tutorials, you can also decide what is comfortable for you.

While most of the crochet tutorials are written for right-handers, left-handers can follow the exact same instructions but in the opposite direction. This also means that when left-handers work in rows, the first row will be worked into the foundation chain beginning from the left side and ending at the right. As a left-hander, this is natural. When working with rounds, you will be crocheting clockwise compared to right-handers who will work counter-clockwise.

How to Crochet Chain Left-Handed

In this chapter, we will learn to crochet the three most basic crochet stitches which include the chain, single crochet, and double crochet, all using the left hand. More types of stitches can be learned online using various tutorials and videos.

1. Start with a slip knot.

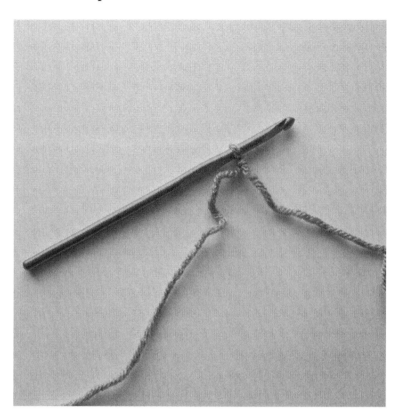

2. As usual, start with your yarn over. Each time you yarn over, you are scooping the yarn clockwise with your hook to pick up the yarn.

2. Draw your hook through the loop. Here you will loop the yarn clockwise.

From here on, repeat steps one, two, and three. Take note that each repetition is one chain.

How to Single Crochet Left-Handed

1. Begin by crocheting a foundation chain with the length of your choice.

2. Now, insert your hook into the second chain that is to the right of the hook. Always make sure your hook is in your left hand, and the chain extends out to the right hand.

3. In the image above, it shows how you will get into the chain using your hook, and you also have two loops on top of the hook and one below. Yarn over.

4. Next, draw a loop through, and now you will see two loops on your hook at the end of this step.

5. Yarn over again.

6. When you are at this step, pull your hook through both loops. Now you have made your very first (sc) or single crochet. Well done!

7. Now all you need to do is insert your hook into the very next chain and repeat steps three through six. Thereafter, repeat step seven across the row.

How to Double Crochet Left-Handed

1. To start this, you need to create a set of foundation chains according to the length of your choice, or according to the pattern. These are the same steps a right-handed crocheter would follow.

2 Yarn over.

3. Now, insert your hook into the fourth chain which is located towards the right, because you are working from the left of your hook.

4. Now, yarn over again.

5. In this step, you need to draw your hook through the loop. Here, you will notice three loops on your hook when you reach the end of the step.

6. Now yarn over and then draw your hook through the first two of those three loops on the hook.

7. Next, yarn over again and here, you need and draw your hook through the two loops. Congratulations, you have now completed your first ever double crochet as a left-handed!

To continue your double crochet, begin with doing a yarn over and then insert the hook into the next stitch. You should repeat steps four to seven, followed by repeating step eight across row.

From here on, yarn over and insert your crochet hook into the next stitch.

If you observe the photo above, it shows that you are starting your next stitch into the third chain of the turning chain from the row before. This is done to ensure that the stitch count remains correct and the shape is not triangular. Next, all you need to do is repeat your (dc) stitches across the entire row.

Tips for Left-Handed Crochet

- When you leave your beginning yarn tail hanging at the beginning of each project, do not crochet over the tail.

- When a pattern mentions either the right side or the wrong side, look for the tail as a cue. The right side will always be where the tail is on the bottom right corner.

- Each time you yarn over, simple scoop the yarn clockwise. This is especially crucial when you are a beginner. Both written and visual patterns can be achieved using left-handed crocheters. You can always reverse images with charts and graphs. Once you have reversed the image, you may use it as a guide.

How to Adapt Patterns to Left-Handed Crochet

Rest assured if you think there aren't enough left-handed crochet patterns, we have a simple solution for you. Just about any straightforward crochet pattern can be followed the way it is written. All left-handed crocheters need to do is reverse the direction that they are working in.

However, some patterns need to be reversed properly so that they work the same way they do in their original form. In tapestry crochet for example and most crochets that require colorwork, you will need to reverse the pattern.

Otherwise, you will end up with a reversed image that looks backwards. For instance, words could end up spelled backwards.

If a right-handed crocheter worked the pattern with odd rows from right to left, the left-handed crocheter would need to work on them from right to left.

Most symbol charts are written for right-handers, so if you are using a symbol chart, use the same number of stitches but work in the opposite direction. You just need to mirror the chart.

Some people can reverse this pattern in their head, but this takes time and requires experience. It's okay if you cannot do this. All you need to do is create a mirror image of the pattern for yourself, so technically, you can use any graph, symbol, or chart and reverse it. You can do this by using photo editing tools that will automatically reverse the instructions. You can also do this by using an actual mirror to reverse the image.

For written patterns, go through the pattern instructions and highlight the cues indicating the direction to work towards. If you see instructions such as, "connect yarn to right corner," or "work into the wrong side of the work," this would mean that you need to reverse the instruction in your head or write your notes on it, so you don't forget. So, your instructions would be joining the yarn to the left corner or working on the right side of the project.

Chapter 6:
Tips and Tricks to Crocheting

Every crocheter requires tips and tricks to become a pro. These tips and tricks help make things easier when you begin crocheting.

Crocheting Using Thread

When it comes to crocheting thread, remember that smaller is bigger. Threads are labeled according to their thickness. The thicker the thread, the smaller is the number. It is counterintuitive, but the more you crochet, the more you will get used to it.

- As a beginner, you can always start with a crochet thread three, then move up to a five and ten. Size twenty or thirty threads can be used once you have built up your skills.

- As with the crochet threads, follow the same approach with steel crochet hooks. The smaller the size, the bigger the crochet hook. You can also look at the mm size that is usually printed on the hook itself. For example, a hook sized nine is 1.25 mm while the hook sized ten is 1.15 mm.

- As a beginner, you should start with a hook size that the pattern calls for. Once you have honed your skills a little more, you can adjust your hooks based on your comfort level and gauge.

- For beginners, it is always good to use steel crochet hooks. These hooks are much easier to use when it comes to working with thread.

- People often find crocheting using thread more difficult compared to using yarn, and it is only because of the thinner hooks involved. When you are working with the thread, all you need to do is choose a hook that has a bigger handle - that's all!

- When purchasing thread, always buy a crochet thread and steer clear from embroidery or sewing thread. Although you can crochet with almost anything that resembles yarn or thread, you can make your life easier by sticking to the kind of thread that is meant for crocheting.

- When you work with yarn overs, make sure to work closely with the crochet hook head. You always want to ensure that the work on the hook is done above the section of the hook where it starts to get wider.

  Otherwise, your loops will be extremely loose.

- Another tip would be to thread around your non-crocheting hand, so it is easier to control your tension. This is extremely helpful when thread crocheting.

Crocheting Hacks with Yarn

- To prevent the balls of yarn from falling and rolling away while you are crocheting, put them in a hand wipe container. Just make sure to wash and clean it first. The yarn can be pulled through the hole of the hand wipe container.

- Use bobby pins or safety pins, or even a paper clip to mark your rows, or stitch a colored yarn or thread into the valley of the first stitch. Bobby pins and paper clips can be pulled out later once you are done.

- Use pencil boxes or jewelry boxes, or even a toothbrush holder to store your hooks. Food containers and snack containers can also do the trick.

- Using *Excel* sheets to map out your patterns. This is a great way to keep track of where you left off when your crocheting gets interrupted. You can also make the pattern larger to decrease eye strain.

- To figure out the amount of yarn or thread needed for a certain project, calculate the number of rows you can get out of one skein/ball, then determine how many rows your project requires. Then, divide the number of rows the project requires with the number of rows your ball gives you. You will be able to calculate how much yarn is needed this way.

- If you are worried about purchasing too much colored yarn that you won't be using in the future, just buy white washable yarn and dye it according to the pattern's colors.

- To keep your project in place, use yarn needles instead of hooks to weave the ends back through. This holds the project better and eliminates the chances of the yarn traveling.

- Dip the end of the yarn in clear nail polish to make it go through the eye of a needle. When you dip it, twist the yarn tight while it dries.

- Instead of ironing your projects, which is not always ideal, mix water and starch in equal parts and spray liberally on your project. Leave to dry on a flat surface.

- To store patterns in a three-ring notebook, use sheet protectors.

- Keeping an index card with the lists of hooks and yarns you have is a great way to keep inventory. This ensures that the next time you are short of crochet supplies, you already know what you need.

- Yarns and other unfinished projects can be kept in zipper bags.

- It is always a good idea to keep foldable sewing scissors so that they don't snag in your crocheting bag.

- When in doubt, sew more tightly with string than you would with yarn. Try not to stitch so firmly that you hurt your hands. Knit somewhat more firmly than normal (except if you're now a skilled crocheter, at that point, simply do what you generally do!).

- Pay attention to the steps you're about to follow before you figure with thread crochet. Jumping from an okay hook size, labored with a cumbersome yarn all the way down to thread crochet can make your thread paintings appear unbearably tiny. Steadily work your way down to the smaller sizes.

- Always do your crochet work in good light so that you don't strain your eyes. This also makes crocheting easier. This is the same reason why, as beginners, you need to work with a lighter colored thread as it makes it easier for you to find those little stitches.

- Crocheting is fun! Sure, it does have its own challenges, but that's only something you'll need to overcome at the beginning. Learning takes time, so be patient with yourself and enjoy each project you work on.

- Always choose beginner patterns when you're starting off. This will make it easier for you to learn how to combine stitches and learn the ropes of crocheting.

- Working with a simple crochet swatch that uses basic stitches is always ideal, simply to get the best results, minus the pressure of going through with a pattern.

Chapter 7:
Choosing a Crochet Pattern

For beginners, you want to choose a crochet pattern that is easy, but also one that's fun to work with. Once you are comfortable with your skills, you can upgrade to more advanced patterns. As a beginner, you want to take baby steps and enjoy the crocheting process instead of becoming overwhelmed with an advanced pattern and get discouraged. This might cause you to give up on your crocheting journey altogether. There are plenty of beautiful crochet patterns to try for beginners. One way to identify what would work best for you is to look at the crochet pattern schematic.

Understanding the Crochet Pattern

When you have chosen a pattern, the next thing to do is to read the instructions entirely, which also includes the stitch guide, any notes that come with it, the diagrams, charts, and the finishing sections. Confusion can be avoided by reading these notes. You will also find plenty of information on tips and techniques, construction, guidelines for keeping track of your stitches, as well as what to do with scrap yarn. As a beginner, you will seek immense knowledge by going through the stitch guide and identifying the kinds of stitches that you have never tried before.

Gauge Swatch

The gauge swatch is very important for beginners, although it is often considered the least interesting part of crocheting. Despite its unpopular reputation, the gauge swatch will help you determine the size of your final product.

The gauge swatch is important, especially if you are substituting yarn with all yarns having the same size or weight. When you use substituted yarn, along with the individual crochet tension that goes with it, you may not always end up with the exact gauge with your hook size. If you end up with a wrong or different gauge size, try using a smaller or larger hook depending on your project. This tiny step can make a huge difference to your overall project.

Substituting Yarn in Crochet Patterns

When you do decide to substitute the yarn specified in your pattern, you would need to look for the correct yarn size. If your pattern calls for worsted weight yarn, then look for another type of worsted weight yarn. This does not mean that your yarn size will be correct, but it may require you to play around with different hook sizes to get the right gauge.

Wraps per inch are the best indicator of correct yarn size substitute. *Wraps per inch* or (wpi), can be found by wrapping the yarn continuously around a ruler and then counting the number of wraps you can make in an inch. Keep the fiber content in mind when you substitute yarn. Silk and cotton often have a different drape compared to animal fiber such as wool or alpaca. Pure silk and cotton also have a stretch, and it can 'grow' over time. You can also use acrylic blends or even acrylic yarn as alternatives to animal or plant fibers.

A final note to any beginner is to always believe in your pattern. Anyone attempting this for the first time is bound to hit a number of road bumps and dead ends, and it is the same for you and your crocheting. Even designers are always pushing the envelope and discovering new techniques for stitch textures and unique constructions, so this should not discourage you from completing an easy crocheting pattern that you love. Sometimes, the most confusing sections of a crochet pattern for both beginners and even advanced crocheters is understanding the pattern, but as you work on them, it will become much clearer.

It may sound a bit overwhelming, but once you have a firm understanding of how to read crochet patterns, everything will become a lot easier. Always start with something that is easier to understand and meant for beginners.

Chapter 8:
Easy and Fun Crochet Patterns for Beginners

As a beginner, finding easy and fun patterns for your first few projects are crucial for starting your crochet journey. This will help you get the hang of reading patterns, improve hand-eye coordination between the yarn, the hook and the stitches, and most importantly, it will allow you to build enough confidence to get through the entire project. Once you have finished it, you may move on to more advanced patterns in due time. Whether you are crocheting as a hobby, or wish to make Christmas gifts for everybody, the patterns described in this section are great for beginners and are an excellent way to kickstart your crocheting journey.

Small Things

1. Simple Bow

Are you itching to start a quick and easy project? Are you looking for useful crochet projects that will make use of those scrap yarns? I've got you covered! The next few pages are filled with small projects like a coin purse, a bow, motifs, and more.

This project will surely add character and a personalized touch to any hair tie, headband, a shirt, a beanie, a denim jacket, or on a present.

Note: *This works well with any kind of yarn, just make sure you use the appropriate hook according to the yarn's thickness.*

1st Row

1. Make 12 Chains.

2nd to 22nd Row

1. Make 12 DCs on top of the previous row.

How to Assemble

1. Sew both the 1st and 22nd rows together.
2. Lay it flat with the seam in the middle.

3. Pinch the middle with your thumb and index finger and loop the remaining yarn around the strip to form a bow.
4. Secure the yarn at the pack of the bow, fasten in place, and tuck off the ends.

2. Crochet Scrunchie

This lovely, personalized scrunchie will be a great gift for your female friends and family members.

Note: *This works well with any kind of yarn, just make sure you use the appropriate hook according to the yarn's thickness. Here, I suggest a light cotton 3-ply thread.*

1st Round

1. Make a slip knot into the ponytail band. Work your 1st SC.
2. Make 3 Chains, then SC into the band.
3. Repeat step 2 until you've covered the entire band. Allow them to overlap each other to hide the band completely.
4. When completely covered, Slip stitch into your 1st stitch.

2nd Row

1. SC into the 1st Chain Space you come across.
2. Chain 3 and SC into the Chain Space of 3.
3. Repeat step 2 until you've gone through each Chain Space of 3.
4. Slip stitch into your 1st stitch.

3rd Round

1. Slipstitch into the nearest Chain Space and make Chain 3. Make 5 DCs into the same Chain Space, then SC into the next Chain Space.
2. Make 6 DCs into the next Chain Space, and then 1 SC into the next Chain Space.
3. Repeat step 2 until you've reached your 1st stitch for this round. Fasten it off and tuck in ends.

3. Rainbow Fold-Over Coin Purse

Easy, simple, and
eye catching—talk
about aesthetical
and functional.
Have fun making
this in rainbow
shades, gradient
shades, or
alternate between
your favorite colors.

Note: *This works well with any kind of yarn, just make sure you use the appropriate hook according to the yarn's thickness.*

1st Round

1. Make a Magic Ring.
2. Make 3 Chains and 12 DCs into the Magic Ring.
3. Slip stitch into the 1st stitch you made and fasten off. You should have 13 stitches in total.

2nd Round

Change yarn color.

1. Make a DC into one of the stitches from the previous row. Pass in a 2nd DC into the same stitch.
2. Finish this round by making 2 DCs in each stitch from the previous round.
3. Slip stitch into the 1st stitch you made and fasten off. You should have 26 DCs in total.

3ʳᵈ Round

Change yarn color.

1. Start with 1 DC into any stitch from the previous round.
2. In the next stitch, make 2 DCs into the same stitch, and make 1 DC in the next stitch.
3. Repeat step 2 until you finish this round, alternating between 2 DCs and 1 DC.
4. Slip stitch into your 1ˢᵗ stitch and fasten off. You should have 39 DCs.

4ᵗʰ Round

Change yarn color.

1. Make two DCs in two separate stitches.
2. Make 2 DCs into one stitch.
3. Repeat steps 1 and 2 until you finish this round, alternating between 2 DCs in two separate stitches and one 2 DCs in the same stitch.
4. Slip stitch into the 1ˢᵗ stitch you made and fasten off. You should have 52 DCs.

5ᵗʰ Round

Change yarn color.

1. In this round, make 3 DCs in three separate stitches, and stitch in 2 DCs into the 4th stitch.
2. Keep alternating between 3 DCs in three separate stitches, and stitch in 2 DCs into the 4th stitch
3. Slipstitch into the first stitch you made and fasten off. You should have 65 DCs.

6th Round

Change yarn color.

1. In this round, make 4 DCs in three separate stitches, and stitch in 2 DCs into the 5th stitch.
2. Keep alternating between 4 DCs in three separate stitches, and stitch in 2 DCs into the 5th stitch
3. Slipstitch into the first stitch you made and fasten off. You should have 78 DCs.

7th Round

Change yarn color.

1. In this round, make 5 DCs in three separate stitches, and stitch in 2 DCs into the 6th stitch.
2. Keep alternating between 5 DCs in three separate stitches, and stitch in 2 DCs into the 6th stitch
3. Slipstitch into the first stitch you made and fasten off. You should have 91 DCs.

How to Assemble

1. With a needle and thread, sew in a zipper on half of the circle.
2. Fold over, and sew in the other half onto the other side of the zipper.
3. Embellish with beads and sequins or leave as is.

4. Tube Pencil Case

We all could use a cute pencil case! Try making this convenient and easy-to-fashion pencil case for yourself or a loved one.

Note: *This works well with any kind of yarn, just make sure you use the appropriate hook according to the yarn's thickness.*

You will need

- Needle
- Button

We will be working around this project in a spiral, so no need to make a slip stitch after every round.

1st Round

1. Make a Magic Ring.
2. Make 6 SCs into the Magic Ring.

2nd Round

1. Make 2 SCs in each stitch from the previous round. You should have 12 SCs in total.

3rd Round

1. Make 2 SCs in one stitch, then follow up with 2 SCs in two stitches.
2. Repeat step 1 until you finish this round. You should have a total of 18 SCs.

4th Round

1. SC the back loop only of each stitch from the previous round, maintaining 18 SCs throughout each round. Repeat this step until you get to your desired length.

Closure Flap

1st Row

2. Chain 1 and then turn your work over.
3. Make 7 SCs

2nd to 5th Row

1. Repeat 1st row.

6th Row

2. Chain 1 then turn your work over.
3. Make 2 SCs into the next 2 stitches, then Chain 3, skip 3 stitches, and finally SC into the last 2 stitches.

7th Row

1. Make 1 Chain and SC through all 7 stitches from the previous row.
2. Now slowly keep making SCs around the flap and the rim of the pencil case to make it look neat. Slip stitch, fasten off, and tuck in the ends.

Position the button and sew in place. Fasten off and tuck in the ends.

5. African Flower Hexagon

This is one of the most versatile patches you will find in the history of crochet. If you join them together, you can create unique things like stuffed animals, blankets, pillowcases, balls, purses, and so much more. The trick to it is to use random colors to make it brighter and eye catching. This is a good way to make use of scrap yarns.

The pattern is pretty straightforward and easy to do. Connecting it together and experimenting with ideas is what will creativity and style.

Note: *This works well with any kind of yarn, just make sure you use the appropriate hook according to the yarn's thickness.*

1st Row

1. Start with a Magic Ring.
2. Chain 3 (this will be considered as your 1st DC) and next to it, make a DC, and then a Chain.
3. Make five more sets of 2 DCs and one Chain stitch. You will end up with 6 in total.
4. After your last Chain, slip stitch into your first DC (the 3 Chains).

2nd Row

This will be a good time to change colors.

1. Fasten off into the first Chain to your left.
2. This row will consist of Chain-centered fan stitches. Having said that, Chain 3, DC into the Chain Space, Chain 1, 2 DCs into the same Chain Space. Continue until you have 6 of these around your circle. One set for each Chain from the previous row.
3. End this row by slip stitching into your first stitch.

3rd Row

1. Fasten off into the first Chain to your left.
2. Now create a full fan of 7 DCs. 1st fan should consist of 3 Chain and 6 DCs. Make 6 of these, 1 set for each Chain from the previous row.
3. And like before, end this row with a slip stitch to your first stitch.

4th Row

This will be a good time to change colors again.

1. This row will consist of SCs. Fasten off into the second DC from the previous row.
2. Start making your SCs around the previous row's DCs.
3. When you reach where the fans of the previous row meet, make a long stitch, going through all the way to where the fans from the 2nd row meet.
4. Continue your SCs around the fans, do not forget to make a long stitch where the fans meet.
5. When you've gone all around the flower, slip stitch into your 1st stitch.

5th Row

This is another time to change colors if you please.

1. Make SCs around the flower again, but this time, only in the back loops.
2. Take off from your last stitch you had left off, make 3 SCs, and when you reach the "corner" of the hexagon (which is the 4th stitch from the previous row, in other words, the center of the "petal"), make a Chain before making another SC in the same stitch.
3. Keep making SCs on the back loops of the previous row, remembering that when you reach the center stitch of the "petal" you need to make a Chain, and then make a SC again in the same loop the last stitch was in.

6. African Flower Pin Cushion

Are you tired of that old tomato pin cushion? Make your sewing kit bright and cheerful with this lovely project.

Note: *This works well with any kind of yarn, just make sure you use the appropriate hook according to the yarn's thickness.*

How to Assemble

1. Make two African Flower Hexagons (*pattern in this book*).
2. Sew on buttons in the center of both African Flower Hexagons.
3. SC both their edges together. Just before you're about to close the seam, stuff it with polyester filling to make it puff up.
4. Continue your SC until it's fully closed.
5. Slip stitch into your 1st stitch.
6. Fasten off and tuck the ends away.

7. Classic Granny Square

Whether you're a newbie or a pro, every crocheter must know this pattern! This motif is as versatile as the African Flower Hexagon, but this one is a go-to patch for making basic yet beautiful afghans.

Note: *This works well with any kind of yarn, just make sure you use the appropriate hook according to the yarn's thickness.*

It is important to check tension and maintain even stitches.

1st Row

1. Start with a Magic Ring.
2. Chain 3 and make 2 DC in the Magic Ring.
3. Chain 2, and make 3 DC in the Magic Ring. Repeat 2 more times until you have 4 sets, forming a roundish square.
4. Slip stitch into your 1st stitch. You should have 12 DC stitches in total.

2nd Row

1. Turn your work over and in the Chain Space you made in 1st row, Chain 3, then make 2 DCs.
2. Chain 2 and make 3 DCs in the same Chain Space.
3. Chain 1 and make 3 DC in the next Chain Space.

4. Repeat steps 2 and 3 until you finish the whole row.
5. Slip stitch into your 1st stitch for this row.

3rd Row

1. Turn your work over and Chain 3 and make 2 DCs into the 1st Chain 2 space from the previous row.
2. Chain 2 and make 3 DCs into the same Chain 2 space.
3. Chain 1 and make 3 DCs into the next Chain Space.
4. Repeat step 3 once more, and then repeat step 2.
5. Keep doing step 3 and 4 until you complete this row. Finish off with a slip stitch.

You can make this Granny Square as big as you prefer, keeping in mind that you need to CH 2 for every "corner" to accommodate a larger amount of stitches, and to also turn it over after ever row. Again, maintain the tension so that you will not end up with a deformed Granny Square.

You can then join these squares with a tapestry needle to make an afghan, a bag, a trendy top, and a lot more. Your imagination and creativity will flourish with this easy and versatile motif!

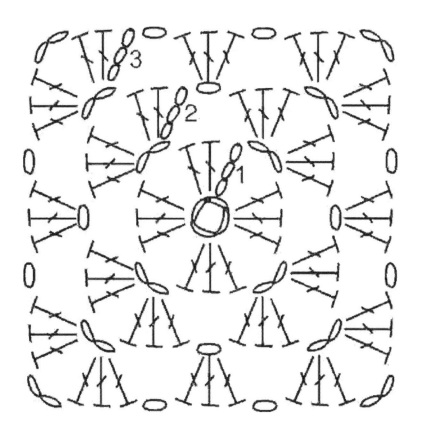

At Home

What makes a house a home? Aside from the people you love, a house becomes a home when you fill it with warm memories, trinkets, and things that you make from the heart. In the next few pages, let your personality and creativity flow in your home, by making these lovely crochet projects designed especially for your home.

1. Granny Crochet Blanket

This is a long-term project. It's easy, but requires a lot of patience and commitment. If you think you're ready to make this gorgeous blanket, then let's get going!

Note: *This works well with any kind of yarn, just make sure you use the appropriate hook according to the yarn's thickness.* It is important to check tension and maintain even stitches.

Here are some things you need to know before starting this project:

- This blanket measures 40in x 69in or 100cm x 175cm
- Each Granny Square should measure 3.5in x 3.5in or 9 x 9cm
- You need to make ***135 Granny Squares*** for this project.

- You need to stitch or crochet together the motifs in 15 rows of 9

Sample steps on how to connect the squares:
1st Round

1. Connect joining yarn with a slip stich in any corner Chain Space with Chain 3, 2 DCs, Chain 3, and 3 DCs. In the same corner Chain Space, Chain 1
2. Make 3 DCs, and Chain 1 three times, and then make 1 DC in the next corner Chain Space, DC 2 together in the same corner Chain Space and corner Chain Space on next square, and 1 DC in the same corner Chain Space, then Chain 1.
3. Repeat step 2 for each square until you reach the other corner of the blanket.
4. Make 3 DCs, Chain 3, and 3 DCs in the blanket corner Chain Space, Chain 1.
5. Repeat from step 2 to step 4 for each side of the blanket, join with slip stitch in first DC, then fasten off.

2nd Round

1. Connect joining yarn with a slip stitch in any corner Chain Space, Chain 3, 2 DCs, Chain 3, and 3 DCs in same corner Chain Space, Chain 1.
2. Make 3 DCs and Chain 1 until you reach the next blanket corner Chain Space, make 3 DCs, Chain 3, 3 DCs in blanket corner Chain Space, Chain 1
3. Repeat step 2 for each side of the blanket, join with slips stitch in first DC, and then fasten off.

3rd to 4th Round

1. Repeat 2nd Round.

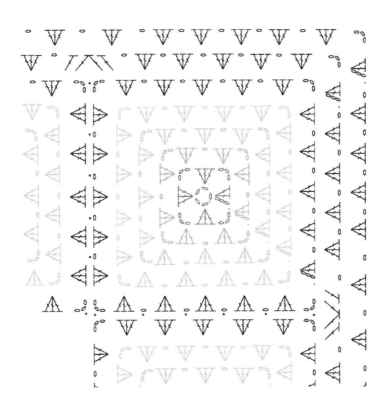

2. Maybelle Flower Coasters

Make these vintage crochet flower motifs into gorgeous coasters. Gradient, variegated, solid, or change colors for every row to make these coasters more personalized.

Note: *For this pattern, I recommend you use a chunky cotton yarn along with an appropriately sized hook.*

1st Round

1. Chain 10 and slip stitch into your 1st stitch to form a circle.
2. Chain 3 this will count as your 1st DC for this round.
3. Make 23 more DCs
4. Then slip stitch into your 1st stitch.

2nd Round

1. Chain 5 then SC into the 3rd stitch from the base of your chain.
2. Repeat step 1 until you finish this row.
3. Slip stitch into the 1st chain you made. You should have 8 half circles in total.

3rd Round

1. Slip stitch into the Chain Space.
2. In the same Chain Space, Chain 3 (this will be your 1st DC) make 1 more DC, Chain 2, 2 more DCs, and 1 Chain.

3. Repeat step 2 into all the Chain Spaces. Changing the 1st Chain 3 into 1 DC.
4. Slip stitch into the 1st stitch you made.

4th Round

1. Slip stitch your way into the 1st Chain Space of 2.
2. In the same Chain Space, Chain 3 and make 6 DCs, and 1 SC into the Chain of 1 from the previous round.
3. Make 7 DCs into the Chain Space of 2, and then 1 SC into the next Chain of 1 from the previous round.
4. Repeat step 4 until you've made fan stitches of 7 DCs into each Chain Space of 2.
5. Slip stitch into your 1st stitch, fasten off, and tuck in ends

3. Simple Mug Cozy

This lovely, simple, and
useful project keeps my
fingers from being burnt
from the hot mug. Make
it for yourself or give it
to someone who is crazy
for hot drinks!

Have fun making this!

Note: *This works well with any kind of <u>cotton</u> yarn, just
make sure you use the appropriate hook for the yarn's
thickness.*

*Size may differ due to your mug's circumference. Measure it
by making enough chains to go around your mug. Keep in
mind that the chain will shrink a little when the SCs are
stitched in.*

1st Row

1. Make 55 Chains.

2nd Row

1. Make 55 SCs on each of the stitches from the previous
   row.

3rd to 7th Row

1. Chain 10, then SC into the 1st stitch.
2. Keep making 55 SCs on each of the stitches from the
   previous row.

8th to 12th Row

1. Chain 10, then SC into the 1st stitch.
2. Keep making 55 SCs on each of the stitches from the previous row.

13th to 14th Row

1. Chain 10, then SC into the 1st stitch.
2. Keep making 55 SCs on each of the stitches from the previous row.

Border

SC around your mug cozy to smoothen out the edges. Fasten off, cut excess yarn and tuck in the ends.

Stitch in 3 buttons—and you're good to go!

4. T-Shirt Yarn Basket

Have you ever worked with T-Shirt yarn before? This will be a great pattern to start off with! Even though this pattern works with any kind of yarn, I suggest you use a T-Shirt yarn.

Note: *This works well with any kind of yarn, just make sure you use the appropriate hook according to the yarn's thickness.* It is important to check tension and maintain even stitches.

1st Round

1. Start with making 3 Chains and slip stitching into the 1st stitch to make a ring.
2. Make 7 SCs into the ring.

2nd Round
1. SC 2 in each stitch. you should have 14 SCs when you finish this round.

3rd Round

1. Alternate making 1 SC in one stitch, and then 2 SCs in one stitch. you should have 21 SCs when you finish this round

4th Round

1. Alternate making 2 SCs in the next two stitches, 2 SCs in one stitch. You should have 28 SCs when you finish this round.

5th Round

1. Alternate making 3 SCs in the next three stitches, 2 SCs in one stitch. You should have 35 SCs when you finish this round.

6th Round

1. Alternate making 4 SCs in the next four stitches, 2 SCs in one stitch. You should have 42 SCs when you finish this round.

7th Round

1. Alternate making 5 SCs in the next five stitches, 2 SCs in one stitch. You should have 49 SCs when you finish this round.

8th Round

1. Make SCs in the back loops of each stitch. You should have 49 SCs when you finish this round.

9th to 16th Round

1. Make SCs around, maintaining 49 stitches for each round.

17th Round

1. Make 22 SCs then Chain 9 to make a handle, skip 3 stitches, SC in the next 21 stitches.
2. Chain 9 and skip 3 stitches again, to make the second handle.

18th Round

1. Continue making SCs around the rim.
2. When you reach the handles, SC over the stitches, making as many as needed to cover over the stitches from the previous round.

3. Slip stitch, fasten off and tuck in the ends.

5. Starburst Hotpad

This is a rather interesting take on boring hotpads. Make a few to spice up the look of your kitchen.

Functional and aesthetically beautiful, this hotpad is quite easy to make.

Note: *This works well with any kind of yarn, just make sure you use the appropriate hook according to the yarn's thickness.*

Reminder:

- ***DO NOT MAKE THESE HOTPADS OUT OF ACRYLIC YARNS. MAKE SURE THE YARN IS MADE OF COTTON.***
- You will need to make ***five*** of these motifs to achieve this hotpot.
- This will be much more eye-catching if each row is made using different colors.

You will need

- 4-ply **Cotton** worsted weight yarn
- Crochet hook G or 5-6mm
- Tapestry needle

1st Row

1. Form a ring by Chaining 5, and slip stitching into your 1st stitch.
2. Chain 3 (this will serve as your first DC), make 3 DCs into the ring—totaling to 4 DCs. After that, Chain 6. Make 3 more sets.
3. Having 4 sets of 4 DCs and 6 Chains, slip stitch the last stitch of your Chain into your 1sr DC.

2nd Row

1. Chain 3 into the previous row's Chain 6, serving again as your 1st DC, make 11 more DCs into the same ring, totaling to 12 DCs.
2. Repeat step 1 until all 4 the Chain 6 from the previous row has a total of 12 DCs each.

3rd Row

You can go around this piece with a SC to make the shape more stable and to also add more color to it.

How to Assemble

Lay side by side, make sure the right side is facing you. Stitch them together in one corner, and so on, until you end up with a beautiful hotpad, same as the one in the picture. Make sure stitches are not visible, and tuck in ends.

Something to Wear

The next few pages are filled with clothing projects for cold winter days or warm summer days. The following projects are fast and easy to make.

1. Classic Puff Stitch Scarf

Make it in a solid color, gradient, or striped! I love crochet scarves, and no one should have just one! Make this scarf for yourself or give it to someone as a gift.

You will need

- 5mm hook
- Medium worsted yarn

1st Row

1. Start by making 26 Chain stitches.
2. Chain 3 and make your 1st Puff Stitch 1 Chain after the base of your Chain 3.
3. Make 12 Puff Stitches in total, with 1 Chain in between each.

2nd Row

1. Chain 3 and Continue making Puff Stitches in between the Puff Stitches from the previous row. Maintain 12 Puff Stitches per row, with 1 Chain in between each.

Keep going until you achieve your desired length.

Remember to always maintain 12 Puff Stitches per row, with 1 Chain in between each.

Add tassels at the end by cutting yarns in an equal length and attaching them by making a Lark's Head knot in the gaps between the Puff Stitches in the bottom ends of the scarf.

2. V-Stitch Infinity Scarf

Like I said, one can never have enough scarves! Try out this versatile scarf pattern. You can either make an infinity scarf or a regular one where you can add tassels. The length can be adjusted to your preference.

You will need

- 5mm hook
- Medium worsted yarn

1st Row

1. Begin by making 25 Chains.
2. DC into the 4th stitch from the hook. Chain 1 and DC into the same stitch to form a V. The 1st 3 Chains is your 1st DC for this row.
3. Skip 1 Chain from the previous row.
4. All in the same stitch, make DC, Chain 1, DC, and skip 1 stitch from the previous row.
5. Repeat step 4 until you finish this row.
6. Make 1 DC into the last Chain from the previous row. You should have 11 V-Stitches and 1 DC on each end of this row.

2nd Row

1. Turn your work over and Chain 3. Make V-Stitches into every V from the previous row, and then make 1 DC into the last stitch.

3rd to 80th Row

1. Repeat the 2nd Row until you reach the 80th Row.
2. To join each end, sew them together by making slip stitches.
3. Fasten off, cut, and tuck in the ends.

Note that this scarf is versatile and can be made as a regular scarf, or as an infinity scarf. It can be as long, or as short as you please. To achieve an infinity scarf, I suggest you make 80 rows or more, depending on your preference.

3. Virus Shawl

This interestingly named shawl pattern is easy and works up fast. There are many speculations, as to why it is named the way it is, but one thing is for certain—it is beautiful.

This pattern looks complicated, but is repetitive in an easy manner. So once you get the hang of it, it starts becoming easier to remember.

Note: *This works well with any kind of yarn, just make sure you use the appropriate hook according to the yarn's thickness.*

1st Row

1. Start with a slipstitch, and then Chain 10.
2. We will make a circle out of this, so link the end of your 10th Chain to the very first one.
3. Chain 3, and then do DC <u>into</u> the circle.
4. You now have 2 stitches. Continue making DCs into the circle until you have 20 DCs in total.

You want your DCs to form a U, and be flat as this is the middle of the triangular shawl pattern. So, bunch them up together and proceed to the 2nd row.

2nd Row

1. Turn your work over to the opposite side.

2. After the last double Chain, make 3 Chains. This will be considered your first DC in the 2nd row.
3. Make a total of 20 DCs on top of the first 20 you made.

3rd Row

1. Now turn your work over, and Chain 4 from the last DC.
2. In this row, we will start adding 1 Chain after each DC. Your 4th Chain will be considered your 1st Chain, as those 3 Chains before that are considered a DC.
3. Keep making DCs and single Chains alternatively until you reach the end of your semi-circle.

4th Row

This is where the pattern will start to emerge and become more interesting.

1. Turn your work over, and Chain 10 from the last DC.
2. Make a SC on the second Chain stitch.
3. Chain 4, and make a SC on the second Chain stitch from your last SC, do this step 3 times.
4. After the last SC, Chain 7 and then single stitch into the second Chain stitch. Make 2 of these.
5. Again, Chain 4, and make a SC on the second Chain stitch from your last SC, do this step 3 times.
6. After the last SC, Chain 7, and end this row with a DC into the last stitch.

5th Row

1. Turn your work over.
2. Make 3 Chain stitches after the DC. This will count as your 1st DC for this row.

3. After that, make 9 DCs into the Chain Space. Totaling to 10 if you count the 3 Chain stitches you made at the beginning.
4. Make a SC into the first small Chain Space, and then Chain 4
5. SC into the next small Chain Space, and Chain 4 again.
6. Make another SC into the last small Chain Space, and DC 10 into the big Chain Space that you come across.
7. After the 10th DC, continue with 10 more into the next big Chain Space.
8. Repeat step 4 and 5.
9. After the last SC, end this row with 10 DCs into the last big Chain Space.

6th Row

1. Turn your work over.
2. From the last DC from the previous row, make 3 Chains.
3. Make 9 DCs on top of the DCs from the previous row. Totaling to 10 DCs if you count the 1st 3 Chains you made.
4. Make a SC on the first small Chain Space, Chain 4, and then make another SC on the next small Chain Space.
5. Make 10 DCs on the previous row's 10 DCs.
6. After the last DC, continue making 10 more DCs on the next 10 DCs of the previous row.
7. Repeat step 4.
8. After that, end this row by making 10 DCs on top of the 10 DCs from the previous row.

7th Row

1. Turn your work over.
4. Same as the beginning of the 3rd row, Chain 4 from the last DC, because in this row, we will start adding 1

Chain after each DC. Your 4th Chain will be considered your 1st Chain, as those 3 Chains before that are considered a DC.

5. Alternately make DCs and Chains until you have 9 Chains and 10 DCs (including the first 3 Chains in the beginning) in total.
6. Repeat step 5 for the next 10 DCs from your previous row.
7. Only for this specific part, add 1 Chain before you repeat step 5 again.
8. End this row by repeating step 5 again.

8th Row

The 8th row will be similar to the 4th row, composed of big and small Chain Spaces to accommodate further expansion of the design.

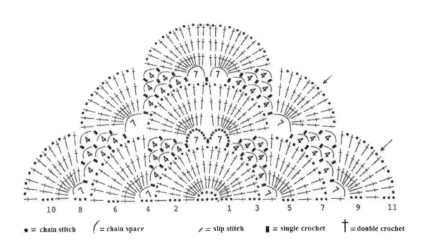

10   8   6   4   2   1   3   5   7   9   11

• = chain stitch   ⌒ = chain space   ╱ = slip stitch   ▌= single crochet   † = double crochet

4. Granny Square Crop Top

Perfect for summer days on the beach! Since crop tops are trending again, I decided to include this pattern for the young and young at heart. This top is perfect to make for yourself, or as a gift to someone.

Note: *This works well with any kind of yarn, just make sure you use the appropriate hook according to the yarn's thickness.*

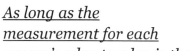

As long as the measurement for each square's edge to edge is the same, it's going to be fine.

You need to make 8 Granny Squares (*pattern found in this book*) that is according to your size (refer to size chart).

Remember to measure the squares edge to edge and not across.

Join the squares together however you like and add fringe by cutting yarns of the same length and attaching them to the bottom by making a Lark's Head knot.

Show off your creativity with this project. Do not be afraid to try new things!

Sizing	S	M	L	XL	XXL
Bust	34-36in	36-38in	40-42in	43-44in	46-48in
To join as is	6in	6.5in	7in	7.5in	8in
w/ Decorative border	5.5in	6in	6.5in	7in	7.5in
Strap Length	12in	13in	14in	15in	16in

5. Puff Stitch Beanie

Just like scarves, you can never have enough crochet beanies! Try making it with gradient or variegated yarn, and if you prefer beanies with big pompoms, you can add that, as well as other embellishments to make it more personalized to give it some color splash and character.

Have fun making this easy project!

1st Row

1. Make a ring with Chain 3, and then slip stitch into the first stitch.
2. In the ring, make 6 puff stitches and then join the last stitch with the 1st puff stitch.

2nd Row

1. In each gap—or Chain 1 spaces from the previous row—make 2 puff stitches in between. Making 12 in total.

3rd Row

2. In the first gap space or Chain 1, make 1 puff stitch, and in the next, make 2 puff stitches. Alternate between making 1 puff stitch, and 2 puff stitches until you finished this row. Having 18 puff stitches in total.

3. Slip stitch into the 1st puff stitch you made for this row.

4th Row

1. Alternate around this row by first making 2 puff stitches in the 1st 2 gaps, and then make 2 puff stitches in the 3rd gap. Alternate this 'two-1, one-2' until you finish this row. Having 24 puff stitches in total.
2. Finish off with a slip stitch.

5th Row

1. Alternate around this row with 1 puff stitch for the first 3 gaps, and then make 2 puff stitches on the 4th gap. Keep making this 'three-1, one-2' pattern until you finish this row. Having 30 puff stitches in total.
2. Slip stitch into the 1st puff stitch you made for this row.

6th Row

1. Alternate around t
2. his row with 1 puff stitch for the first 4 gaps, and then make 2 puff stitches on the 5th gap. Keep making this 'four-1, one-2' pattern until you finish this row. Having 36 puff stitches in total.
3. Slip stitch into the 1st puff stitch you made for this row.

7th to 15th Row

1. This time, only make 1 puff stitch for each gap. Having 36 puff stitches in total.
2. Slip stitch into the 1st puff stitch you made for this row.

16th Row

1. Chain 1, then SC in the 1st puff stitch from the previous row. It would help to put a stitch marker here. SC on each and every stitch from the previous row, including the gaps and the puff stitches. Do not slip stitch into the 1st stitch; instead, continue around until you have 72 SC in total.

17th to 19th Row

Keep making SC into each stitch until you reach the stitch marker on the 19th row.

Slip stitch into the following 2 stitches. Make sure to tuck in the ends.

6. Crochet Bow Ear Warmers

Keep those ears warm and toasty with these stylish ear warmers. The pattern is very straightforward and easy to understand. Try making this for yourself or make it for someone who needs to stay warm and cozy!

You will need:

- Worsted weight yarn or any bulky size 5 yarn
- 6mm Hook

Note: These instructions are for making an adult-sized headband with 20-22 inches circumference when done, and a width of 4 inches. It can be customized easily by removing or adding stitches to achieve the perfect fit.

Gauge: for the correct fit, make sure that for every 4 inches, you have 8 stitches for the right fit.

1st Round

1. Make 44 Chains and slip stitch into the first stitch to form a circle, being careful to not twist the loop.

2nd Round

1. Chain 3 (considering this your 1st DC)
2. Make 43 more DCs into each stitch.
3. Slip stitch into your first stitch in this round.

3rd Round

1. Chain 1 and SC in each and every single stitch.
2. Slip stitch into your 1st Chain for this round.

4th to 8th Round

1. Alternate between the 2nd round and 3rd round steps until you reach the 8th round.
2. When you reach the 8th round, and have slipstitched into your 1st stitch for that round, do not fasten off.

Loop yarn around the seam of the headband 6 times or more, depending on your preference. Slip stitch into the last stitch you made and fasten off. Tuck in loose ends.

7. 6-Size Double Pompom Beanie

This versatile beanie pattern comes in 6 sizes. For preemies, newborns, 3-6 months, toddlers, children, and adults. This does not have to end with a pompom on two sides, you can also just put one at the tip, or embellish with appliqués found in the last chapter of this book. Enjoy!

You will need

- **Worsted weight yarn**
- **5mm hook**
- **Tapestry needle**

For this pattern, the beginning Chains in the beginning of each round will not be counted as stitches.

For Preemies: 4.25" to 5.5"

1st Round

1. Begin by making a Magic Ring.
2. Chain 3 then make 9 DCs in the Magic Ring.
3. Slipstitch into the 1st stitch you made in this round. You should have 9 DCs in total.

2nd Round

1. Chain 3
2. Make 2 DC in each stitch from the previous round.

3. Slipstitch into the 1st stitch you made. You should have 18 DCs in total.

3rd Round

1. Chain 3
2. Make 2 DCs into the same stitch and 1 DC into the next stitch.
3. Repeat step 2 until you finish this round.
4. Slipstitch into the 1st stitch you made. You should have 27 DCs in total.

4th Round

1. Chain 3
2. Make 2 DCs into the same stitch, and 2 DC into the next 2 stitches.
3. Repeat step 2 until you finish this round.
4. Slipstitch into the 1st stitch you made. You should have 36 DCs in total.

5th to 8th Round

1. Chain 3
2. DC around each stitch.
3. You should consistently have 36 DCs

9th Round

1. Chain 1
2. SC into each stitch from the previous round.

Slip stitch into your 1st stitch, fasten off, and tuck in ends.

For Newborns: 4.5" to 6"

1st Round

1. Begin by making a Magic Ring.
2. Chain 3 then make 10 DCs in the Magic Ring.
3. Slipstitch into the 1st stitch you made in this round. You should have 10 DCs in total.

2nd Round

1. Chain 3
2. Make 2 DC in each stitch from the previous round.
3. Slipstitch into the 1st stitch you made. You should have 20 DCs in total.

3rd Round

1. Chain 3
2. Make 2 DCs into the same stitch and 1 DC into the next stitch.
3. Repeat step 2 until you finish this round.
4. Slipstitch into the 1st stitch you made. You should have 30 DCs in total.

4th Round

1. Chain 3
2. Make 2 DCs into the same stitch, and 2 DC into the next 2 stitches.
3. Repeat step 2 until you finish this round.
4. Slipstitch into the 1st stitch you made. You should have 40 DCs in total.

5th to 9th Round

1. Chain 3

2. DC around each stitch.
3. You should consistently have 40 DCs

10th Round

1. Chain 1
2. SC into each stitch from the previous round.
3. Slip stitch into your 1st stitch, fasten off, and tuck in ends.

For 3 to 6 Months: 5.75" to 7.5"

1st Round

1. Begin by making a Magic Ring.
2. Chain 3 then make 11 DCs in the Magic Ring.
3. Slipstitch into the 1st stitch you made in this round. You should have 11 DCs in total.

2nd Round

1. Chain 3
2. Make 2 DC in each stitch from the previous round.
3. Slipstitch into the 1st stitch you made. You should have 22 DCs in total.

3rd Round

1. Chain 3
2. Make 2 DCs into the same stitch and 1 DC into the next stitch.
3. Repeat step 2 until you finish this round.
4. Slipstitch into the 1st stitch you made. You should have 33 DCs in total.

4th Round

1. Chain 3
2. Make 2 DCs into the same stitch, and 2 DC into the next 2 stitches.
3. Repeat step 2 until you finish this round.
4. Slipstitch into the 1st stitch you made. You should have 44 DCs in total.

5th Round

1. Chain 3

2. Make 2 DCs into the same stitch, and 10 DC into the next 2 stitches.
3. Repeat step 2 until you finish this round.
4. Slipstitch into the 1st stitch you made. You should have 48 DCs in total.

6th to 11th Round

1. Chain 3
2. DC into each stitch from the previous round.

12th Round

1. Chain 1
2. SC into each stitch from the previous round.
3. Slip stitch into your 1st stitch, fasten off, and tuck in ends.

For Toddlers: 6.75" to 8.75"

1st Round

1. Begin by making a Magic Ring.
2. Chain 3 then make 10 DCs in the Magic Ring.
3. Slipstitch into the 1st stitch you made in this round. You should have 10 DCs in total.

2nd Round

1. Chain 3
2. Make 2 DC in each stitch from the previous round.
3. Slipstitch into the 1st stitch you made. You should have 20 DCs in total.

3rd Round

1. Chain 3
2. Make 2 DCs into the same stitch and 1 DC into the next stitch.
3. Repeat step 2 until you finish this round.
4. Slipstitch into the 1st stitch you made. You should have 33 DCs in total.

4th Round

1. Chain 3
2. Make 2 DCs into the same stitch, and 2 DC into the next 2 stitches.
3. Repeat step 2 until you finish this round.
4. Slipstitch into the 1st stitch you made. You should have 44 DCs in total.

5th Round

1. Chain 3

2. Make 2 DCs into the same stitch, and 10 DC into the next 10 stitches.
3. Repeat step 2 until you finish this round.
4. Slipstitch into the 1st stitch you made. You should have 48 DCs in total.

6th Round

1. Chain 3
2. Make 2 DCs into the same stitch, and 11 DC into the next 11 stitches.
3. Repeat step 2 until you finish this round.
4. Slipstitch into the 1st stitch you made. You should have 52 DCs in total.

7th Round

1. Chain 3
2. Make 2 DCs into the same stitch, and 12 DC into the next 12 stitches.
3. Repeat step 2 until you finish this round.
4. Slipstitch into the 1st stitch you made. You should have 56 DCs in total.

8th to 13th Round

1. Chain 3
2. DC around each stitch
3. You should consistently have 56 DCs

14th Round

1. Chain 1
2. SC into each stitch from the previous round.
3. Slip stitch into your 1st stitch, fasten off, and tuck in ends.

For Children: 7.5" to 10.25"

1st Round

1. Begin by making a Magic Ring.
2. Chain 3 then make 10 DCs in the Magic Ring.
3. Slipstitch into the 1st stitch you made in this round. You should have 10 DCs in total.

2nd Round

1. Chain 3
2. Make 2 DC in each stitch from the previous round.
3. Slipstitch into the 1st stitch you made. You should have 20 DCs in total.

3rd Round

1. Chain 3
2. Make 2 DCs into the same stitch and 1 DC into the next stitch.
3. Repeat step 2 until you finish this round.
4. Slipstitch into the 1st stitch you made. You should have 30 DCs in total.

4th Round

1. Chain 3
2. Make 2 DCs into the same stitch, and 2 DC into the next 2 stitches.
3. Repeat step 2 until you finish this round.
4. Slipstitch into the 1st stitch you made. You should have 40 DCs in total.

5th Round

1. Chain 3

2. Make 2 DCs into the same stitch, and 3 DC into the next 3 stitches.
3. Repeat step 2 until you finish this round.
4. Slipstitch into the 1st stitch you made. You should have 50 DCs in total.

6th Round

1. Chain 3
2. Make 2 DCs into the same stitch, and 4 DC into the next 4 stitches.
3. Repeat step 2 until you finish this round.
4. Slipstitch into the 1st stitch you made. You should have 60 DCs in total.

7th Round

1. Chain 3
2. Make 2 DCs into the same stitch, and 29 DC into the next 29 stitches.
3. Repeat step 2 until you finish this round.
4. Slipstitch into the 1st stitch you made. You should have 62 DCs in total.

8th to 14th Round

1. Chain 3
2. DC around each stitch
3. You should consistently have 62 DCs

15th Round

1. Chain 1
2. Half DC into each stitch from the previous round.
3. Slip stitch into your 1st stitch, fasten off, and tuck in ends.

For Adults: 8.25" to 11"

1st Round

1. Begin by making a Magic Ring.
2. Chain 3 then make 11 DCs in the Magic Ring.
3. Slipstitch into the 1st stitch you made in this round. You should have 11 DCs in total.

2nd Round

1. Chain 3
2. Make 2 DC in each stitch from the previous round.
3. Slipstitch into the 1st stitch you made. You should have 22 DCs in total.

3rd Round

1. Chain 3
2. Make 2 DCs into the same stitch and 1 DC into the next stitch.
3. Repeat step 2 until you finish this round.
4. Slipstitch into the 1st stitch you made. You should have 33 DCs in total.

4th Round

1. Chain 3
2. Make 2 DCs into the same stitch, and 2 DC into the next 2 stitches.
3. Repeat step 2 until you finish this round.
4. Slipstitch into the 1st stitch you made. You should have 44 DCs in total.

5th Round

1. Chain 3

2. Make 2 DCs into the same stitch, and 3 DC into the next 3 stitches.
3. Repeat step 2 until you finish this round.
4. Slipstitch into the 1st stitch you made. You should have 55 DCs in total.

6th Round

1. Chain 3
2. Make 2 DCs into the same stitch, and 4 DC into the next 4 stitches.
3. Repeat step 2 until you finish this round.
4. Slipstitch into the 1st stitch you made. You should have 66 DCs in total.

7th to 15th Round

1. Chain 3
2. DC around each stitch
3. You should consistently have 66 DCs

16th Round

1. Chain 1
2. Half DC into each stitch from the previous round.
3. Slip stitch into your 1st stitch, fasten off, and tuck in ends.

Pompoms

Make 2 Pompoms that are as fluffy and as thick as you please. The fluffier, the better!

How to Assemble

Stitch two pompoms on either side of the beanie. Make sure it's positioned well before you stitch it in.

Crochet Appliqués

Have fun using all those scrap yarns on the projects we have mentioned in the next few pages! Make these appliqués for your crochet quilts, denim jackets, beanies, scarves, jeans, hair clips, and so much more! The possibilities are as limitless as your creativity.

1. Popcorn Stitch Flower

This easy, cute, and beautiful flower can be linked together to make rugs, headbands, or just for appliqués.

Note: *This works well with any kind of yarn, just make sure you use the appropriate hook according to the yarn's thickness.*

1st Round

1. Make a Magic Ring and SC 10 through it.
2. Slip stitch into the 1st stitch you made.

2nd Round

If you want to change colors for the petals, now is the time to do so.

1. Chain 3 and then make 4 Half DC into the same SC.
2. You should have 5 loops on your hook.

3. Keeping the 5 loops on, continue making 4 more Half DC into the next SC. You should have 9 loops on your hook.
4. Finally, with the yarn over your hook, pull it through all 9 loops on the hook.
5. Chain 3 and slip stitch into the next SC.
6. Repeat this step until you have 5 petals.

2. Classic Rose

This Classic Rose crochet is gorgeous for stitching on the side of a beanie, a denim jacket, on scarves, and so much more!

Note: *This works well with any kind of yarn, just make sure you use the appropriate hook according to the yarn's thickness.*

You will need

- Tapestry needle or any blunt needle.

1st Row

1. Leaving about 12 inches of thread for sewing, make 57 Chains.

2nd Row

1. Make a DC in the 6th chain from your hook, then Chain 2 and DC again into the same stitch.
2. Chain 2 and skip the next 2 Chains from the previous row, then DC, Chain 2, and DC again into the same stitch.
3. Repeat step 2 until you finish this row.

3rd Row

1. Turn your work over. Chain 3, this is considered your 1st DC. Make 5 DCs into the first Chain Space of 2, then make 1 SC into the next Chain Space of 2.
2. DC 6 into the next Chain Space of 2, and then 1 SC into the next Chain space of 2.

3. Repeat step 2 until you get 6 sets of these Fan Stitch of 6 DCs.
4. Now, make 9 DCs into the next Chain Space of 2, then SC into the next Chain Space of 2.
5. Repeat step 4 until you have 5 sets of these Fan Stitch of 9 DCs.
6. Lastly, make 12 DCs in the next Chain Space of 2, then SC one in the next Chain Space of 2.
7. Repeat step 6 until you finish this row off, you should end with a SC in the last Chain Space.
8. Fasten off and leave a good few inches of yarn for assembling.

How to Assemble

Start rolling from the side where there are Fan Stitches of 6. Grab your tapestry needle, and start sewing it together. Keep rolling and sewing until you reach the end of the strip.

Once fully bunched together, tie both ends together tightly and securely. Tuck in the ends, and cut off.

3. Simple Heart Crochet

Here's another easy and beautiful appliqué for your crochet projects. Show some love with this crochet appliqué! This would look great scattered all over a child or a child at heart's jeans, on a beanie, or hair clips.

Note: *This works well with any kind of yarn, just make sure you use the appropriate hook according to the yarn's thickness.*

1st Round

1. Begin with a Magic Ring. Chain 3 and make 15 DCs into the Magic Ring.
2. Slip stitch into your 1st stitch. You should have 16 DCs in total.

2nd Round

1. Chain 2 and 1 DC into the same stitch.
2. Make 4 TRCs into the next stitch, and then 2 DCs into the next stitch.
3. Make 4 Half DC into the next 4 stitches.

We have now reached the bottom point of the heart.

4. Repeat step 3, all the way to step 1.
5. Slip stitch into the same stitch.
6. Fasten off, and tuck in ends.

4. Easy Bear

Are you looking for an easy to make bear for baby blankets, baby hats, baby jeans, or your patchwork afghan? I have the cutest and easiest bear pattern for you.

Note: *This works well with any kind of yarn, just make sure you use the appropriate hook according to the yarn's thickness.*

1st Round

1. Using a black yarn, begin with a Magic Ring.
2. Make 8 SC into the Magic Ring.
3. Slip stitch into the your 1st stitch and fasten off.

2nd Round

1. Using a brown yarn, Chain 3 and make 1 DC on the same SC from the previous round.
2. Make 2 DCs into the next SC, and so on, until you have a total of 16 DCs including the Chain 3.
3. Slip stitch onto the top of your Chain 3

3rd Round

1. Chain 3 and make 1 DC into the same stitch from the previous round.
2. Make 2 DCs into each stitch from the previous round.
3. Repeat step 2 until you have 32 DCs in total.

4th Round

1. Making a fan stitch, DC into the 2nd stitch to the left.
2. Make 6 more DCs into the same stitch to form the 1st ear.
3. SC into the 2nd stitch to the left.
4. SC into 6 more stitches.
5. Make the 2nd ear by making 7 DCs into the second stitch to left.
6. Finish off the second ear, by making a SC into the 2nd stitch to the left.
7. Finish the rest of the round with a SC to each remaining stitches until you reach the base of the 1st ear.
8. Slip stitch into it, and fasten off. Tuck away the ends. Stitch eyes with black yarn.

5. Basic Cherry

Adorable Cherry appliqués? I've got you covered! How adorable would these look on hairclips and anything denim?

Note: *This works well with any kind of yarn, just make sure you use the appropriate hook according to the yarn's thickness.*

Cherry Round

Make 2

1. Using red or any other preferred color, make a Magic Ring and make Chain 2.
2. Make 11 DCs.
3. Slip stitch onto your 1st stitch.
4. Fasten off the Magic Ring and tuck ends.

1st Stem

1. Slip stitch your green yarn into one of the cherry rounds and Chain 8.

1st Leaf

1. Chain 8
2. Flip your work and make 1 SC and 1 DC starting from your 2nd to the last stitch.
3. Make 2 TRCs, 1 DC and then SC.

2nd Leaf

1. Chain 8
2. Flip your work and make 1 SC and 1 DC starting from your 2nd to the last stitch.
3. Make 2 TRCs, 1 DC and then SC.
4. Slip stitch into the base of the 1st Leaf.

2nd Stem

1. Chain 8 and slipstitch into another Cherry round.
2. Fasten off and tuck in ends.

Keep in mind that you need to follow the order of the steps to achieve the look in the picture.

6. Simple Star

Simple with a grand look, this Crochet Star appliqué will be perfect for your next project.

Note: *This works well with any kind of yarn, just make sure you use the appropriate hook according to the yarn's thickness.*

1st Round

1. Chain 5. Make a slip stitch into your 1st stitch to make a ring.

2nd Round

2. Chain 3 and then make 2 DCs into the ring.
3. Chain 1 and make 3 DCs into the ring.
4. Repeat step 2 three more times, until you have 5 sets of 3 DCs with 5 Chain 1 in between.

3rd Round

1. Slip stitch into the next DC.
2. Into the 1st Chain Space to the left, make 2 DCs, 1 TRC, Chain 3, 1 TRC, and 2 DCs. After that, slip stitch into the middle stitch of the 1st set of 3 DCs to the left.
3. Repeat step 2 four more times to achieve a star.

Conclusion

Crocheting is a fun craft to try your hand at. The learning curve is not steep as it only takes a few tries to get the hang of crocheting. Once you start, you will find yourself eager and interested in taking on bigger and more challenging projects. However, even the advanced projects are quite easy to master once you know the basics, so always have fun and if you feel like you've hit a roadblock, don't worry- just look back on this book or the patterns, and you'll be on the right track in no time. Good luck!

Exclusive 5-day bonus course just for you!

We will be sharing top crafting mistakes to avoid, how to save money on supplies and extra craft patterns!

Simply let us know where to send the course e-mails to via this link below.

https://bit.ly/nancy-gordon

For any general feedback & enquiries, you can reach us at bookgrowthpublishing@mail.com

Easy Crocheting Patterns for Beginners

30 Crochet Patterns With Step By Step Instructions That Any Beginners Can Do From Baby Blankets To Amigurumi And Many More

Nancy Gordon

Contents

Additionally, the information in the following pages is intended only for informational purposes and should thus be thought of as universal. As befitting its nature, it is presented without assurance regarding its prolonged validity or interim quality. Trademarks that are mentioned are done without written consent and can in no way be considered an endorsement from the trademark holder.

Introduction

Congratulations on purchasing *Easy Crocheting Patterns For Beginners*! Crocheting is a traditional artform that continues to offer an abundance of fun to everyone who tries it. Many crochet patterns can also fulfill practical purposes, providing you with the opportunity to enjoy your creations in a useful manner, too.

For many years, crochet was used as a staple in the textile industry for creating items such as clothing, blankets, pillows, tablecloths, curtains, and other household products that were used for both decorative and practical purposes. While we now have major mills that provide textiles for people, crocheting is still a fun hobby that many have. In some regions, crocheting continues to be a popular and well-loved craft that provides a purpose, too.

In *Easy Crocheting Patterns For Beginners*, we are going to cover 30 different patterns that you will find great joy in. These patterns will challenge you and help increase your skill level, though they are intended for beginners and will be easy to make no matter how new you are to the craft. If you are ready to push yourself and really start expanding on your skills, I have included a few patterns that are beyond beginner level so that you can learn how to read more complex patterns and develop greater levels of confidence with crocheting.

I encourage you to work your way through this book as a way to help you expand your crocheting abilities. Start by finding a pattern that attracts your attention, and then collect your materials so you can go ahead and make it! You will have a blast.

Chapter 1:
Wearable Accessories

A great way to combine practicality with fun is to create crocheted wearable accessories! With crochet, there are so many different accessories you can create for yourself that are also wearable. For example, hats, scarves, and ponchos! These patterns can keep you warm, help you look stylish, and offer you something to be proud of having made for yourself. They also make wonderful gifts for loved ones, especially since all of these patterns can easily be made into one-size-fits most pattern. Customize your patterns with the favorite colors of your recipients, whether it be yourself of someone else, and you are sure to have a wonderful piece that you can be proud of having made yourself! The bonus? These are all incredibly easy patterns that you can work up, regardless of your skill level.

Hairpin Lace Pirate Toque Pattern

Beginner/Easy

About:

The hairpin toque pattern is a beautiful toque that uses a tassel to offer a flair of style to the top of the toque.

Materials Needed:

4 oz. bulky weight yarn in your color of choice. Hairpin staple 2" wide. Crochet hook size F.

Abbreviations Used:

Chain (Ch)
Single Crochet (Sc)
Slip Stitch (Sl St)

Pattern:

For the Hairpin Lace: Make a loop at the end of your yarn and insert 1 prong of hairpin staple in the loop. Wind your yarn around the right prong of the hairpin staple. Yarn over hook, draw through loop, keeping the loop at the center of the staple. Drop the loop, turn the staple one half turn to the left, then pick up the dropped loop at the center and insert the hook through the top part of the loop on the left hand prong. Pull a loop through, there should now be 2 loops on your hook. Yarn over, and pull it through both of the loops on your hook, completing one Sc. Repeat until there are 64 loops on each side of your staple. Cut the yarn. Work another strip of hairpin lace in the same manner.

Round 1: Attach bulky yarn in 1st 2 loops of 1st strip of hairpin lace. *Ch 2, keep the twist in the loops and Sc through next 2 loops of hairpin lace. Go through both loops at the same time. *Repeat from* to * across the stip. Ch 2, join to 1st Sc with Sl St. (This makes lower edge of your hat).

Round 2: Ch 1, working through back loop of stitches only, 1 Sl St in each Sc and Ch across. Join with Sl St.

Round 3: Working through back loop of stitches only, 1 Sl St in each Sl St. Join. Cut yarn. Sew center of hairpin lace together.

Round 4: Attach bulky yarn in first 2 loops on the opposite side of the same strip. *Ch 2, keep the twist in the loops and Sc through next 2 loops of hairpin lace. Go through both loop´s at the same time. *Repeat from * to * around. Ch 2. Join with Sl St.

Round 5: Join strips as follows: Sl St in next Ch 2 space. Ch 1, Sc through first 2 loops of second strip. Ch 1, Sl St in next Ch 2 space of first strip. *Ch 1, Sc through next 2 loops of 2nd strip, Ch 1, Sl St in next Ch 2 space of first strip. * Repeat from * to * around, ending with Ch 1. Join with Sl St. Cut the yarn. Work another strip of hairpin lace.

Round 6: Attach bulky yarn through first three hoops at the top of the second strip. *Ch 2, Sc, through next 3 loops of hairpin lace. * Repeat from * to * around, Ch 2 and join. Work another strip of hairpin lace.

Round 7: Attach bulky yarn through first three loops at the top of the third strip of hairpin lace. * Ch 2, Sc through next 3 loops of hairpin lace. * Repeat from * to * around. Ch 2, Join with Sl St.

Round 8: Sl St into Ch 2 space and join fourth strip to third strip the same way you did the first two strip. Cut the yarn. Attach bulky yarn though the first four loops at the top of the fourth strip of hairpin lace. *Ch 1, Sc through next 4 loops of hairpin lace. * Repeat from * to * around, Ch 1, Join with Sl St. Cut yarn with a long tail, then thread the yarn through a needle and draw the top of your hat together. Keep the tail long.

For the Tassel: Wind yarn around 4¼ inch cardboard 25 times. Use a small piece of yarn to tie end so all of the loops are tied together. Cut the yarn on the opposite end of the cardboard length. Tie it again approximately ¾" down from the first knot. Trim the tassel evenly, then sew it on to the tip of your hat. Turn the top over about 4" and sew the tassel to the side of your hat so it stays in place.

Vintage Skull Cap

Beginner/Easy

About:

This skull cap is a petite cap that just fits over the top of your head as a way to keep you warm, while also looking stylish. It is an excellent hat or toque for anyone who is looking for something that is not too bulky, and that will still serve excellent warmth.

Materials needed:

3 weight yarn in 3 different colors designated as A, B, and C. Crochet hook size D.

Abbreviations Used:

Chain (Ch)
Single Crochet (Sc)
Slip Stitch (Sl St)

Pattern:

Pattern starts at the tip. Ch 10 with color C.

Round 1: Sc in 3rd Ch from hook. Sc in each of the next 6 Ch spaces. 10 Sc in last Ch. Sc in 10th Sc from hook. Have the point forward, toward you. 2 Sc in each Sc around until you have 21 Sc total in the round.

Round 2: Sc in each Sc around. Sl St to join.

Round 3: *Sc in next Sc, 2 Sc in next Sc (one increase made.) *Repeat from * to * around. Sl St to join.

Round 4: Sc in each Sc around. Sl St to join.

Round 5: *2 Sc in next Sc, Sc in each of next 2 Sc. * Repeat from * to * around. Sl St to join.

Round 6: Sc in each Sc around. Sl St to join.

Round 7: *2 Sc in next Sc, Sc in each of next 3 Sc. * Repeat from * to * around. Sl St to join.

Round 8: Sc in each Sc around. Sl St to join. Drop color C to back of work.

Round 9: Attach color A. Sc in each Sc around. Sl St to join. Drop color A to back of work.

Round 10: Attach color B. Sc in each next 2 Sc. *2 Sc in next Sc. Sc in each of next 4 Sc. * Repeat from * to * around. Sl St to join.

Round 11: Sc in each Sc around. Sl St to join.

Round 12: Sc in each of the next 3 Sc. *2 Sc in next Sc, Sc in each of next 7 Sc. * Repeat from * to * around. Sl St to join.

Round 13: Attach color A. Sc in each Sc around. Sl St to join. Drop color A to back of work.

Round 14: Pick up color C. Work Sc in next Sc. *2 Sc in next Sc. Sc in each of next 5 Sc. * Repeat from * to * around. Sl St to join.

Round 15: Sc in each Sc around. Sl St to join. Drop color C to back of work.

Round 16: Pick up color A. Sc in each of next 3 Sc. *2 Sc in next Sc. Sc in each of next 7 Sc. *Repeat from * to * around. Sl St to join. Drop A to the back.

Round 17: Attach color B. Sc in each Sc around. Sl St to join.

Round 18: Sc in each of next 3 Sc. *2 Sc in next Sc. Sc in each of next 7 Sc. * Repeat * to * around. Sl St to join. Drop color B to the back.

Remaining Rounds: With color A, Sc in each Sc until work measures 6 ½" from tip to edge of work.

Final Round: Sc in base of each Sc around. Sl St to join. Cut off and fasten in your end.

Sport Scarf

Beginner/Easy

About:

This scarf offers both style and functionality, being that it is a chunky warm scarf that is sure to keep you cozy during the cooler months. Although this scarf is big and bold, it is an incredibly easy pattern to create. You will love designing this piece for yourself, or a loved one!

Materials needed:

7 skeins of 4 weight yarn. 5 skeins of color A, 2 skeins of color B. Crochet hook size E.

Abbreviations Used:

Chain (Ch)

Pattern:

Ch 61.

The row: *Wrap yarn around hook, insert hook into next stitch, wrap yarn around hook, pull yarn through, wrap around hook, pull it through all three loops on the hook. One loop remaining. *Repeat * to * across. Ch 1, turn.

Complete the row to create the following pattern:

17 rows of color A

2 rows of color B

3 rows of color A

3 rows of color B

3 rows of color A

4 rows of color B

50 inches of color A

4 rows of color B

3 rows of color A

3 rows of color B

3 rows of color A

2 rows of color B

17 rows of color A

To create your fringe, cut 8 inch strands of color A and color B yarn. Use 3 strands of color A and 3 strands of color B, fold them in half, insert the fold into a stitch on the end of your scarf and pull the ends through the loop. Pull tight and repeat on every 3rd stitch until you have fringe across both ends.

Scarf Collar

Beginner/Easy.

About:

This scarf collar creates a beautiful kerchief-style scarf that will provide both warmth and style to any outfit you are wearing. Because of its smaller size, this pattern works up much faster. You can easily create it in as little as one single afternoon!

Materials Needed:

3 weight yarn, one ball in color A and one ball in color B. Crochet hook in size D. Two snap fasteners.

Abbreviations Used:

Chain (Ch)
Slip Stitch (Sl St)
Single Crochet (Sc)
Double Crochet (Dc)

Pattern:

In Color A, Ch 19. Turn.

Row 1: Sl St in 7th Ch from hook. *Ch 3, skip 2 Ch stitches, Sl St in the next stitch. *Repeat * to − 3 more times. Ch 6, turn.

Row 2: Dc in 4th Ch from hook. Skip Sl St and Ch loop. Dc in next Sl St space. * Ch 3, Dc in Dc just made, Dc in next Sl St. Repeat from * to * 3 more times. Make last Dc in 3rd Ch of turning Ch. (5 patterns made.) Ch 3, turn.

Row 3: Dc in 1st Dc, *Ch 3, Dc in Dc just made, Dc in next Dc from previous row. * Repeat from * to * 4 more times. Ch 6, turn.

Row 4: Dc in 4th Ch from hook, skip 1st Dc of previous row, Dc in next Dc, *Ch 3, in Dc just made, Dc in next Dc from previous row. *Repeat from * to * 3 more times. Ch 2, Sc in Dc just made, Dc in turning Ch 3 space after row 2 (an increase has been made.) Ch 5, turn.

Row 5: Sc in 3rd Ch from hook. Skip 1st Dc of previous row, Dc in next Dc, *Ch 3, Dc in Dc just made. Dc in next Dc of previous row. *Repeat from * to * 4 more times. Ch 6, turn.

Row 6: Dc in 4th Ch from hook. Skip 1st Dc, Dc in next Dc from previous row. *Ch 3, Dc in just made. Dc in next Dc. *Repeat from * to * 4 more times. Ch 3, turn 1 pattern has been increased on the side that will be on the neck edge.

Repeat 3rd, 4th, 5th and 6th rows in order, till there are 22 patterns in the row. For every repetition of these 4 rows, repeat the portion between the *'s one additional time care for increases.

Next, work 10 rows straight. Make Ch 3 loops to finish the outer and neck edges of collar.

Trimming: Attach color B at the right-angle corner, and work along last row as follows: Ch 6, Dc in 4th Ch from hook, Dc in place where Ch 6 started. *Dc in next Dc, Ch 3, Dc in Dc just made, make another Dc in the same Dc from previous row. *Repeat from * to * until you reach the corner. In the corner, make 2 patterns, then continue along other side. At next corner break and fasten thread. Attach color B in 4th row from last, and work another trimming row, parallel to first trimming row. Drape around neck as illustrated and sew on snap fasteners. Sew on buttons with color B.

Striped Poncho

Beginner/Easy.

About:

This striped poncho creates a beautiful poncho that will drape over any figure. It is warm, stylish, and makes for a wonderful present for yourself or someone else. Although this is a larger project and it will require more commitment from you, it is not a project that will require a large amount of skill. Instead, it allows your beginner-level skills to be put to work to make something truly magnificent. This poncho will take a few days to make, at least, but once you are done you will be proud of the piece you have created.

Materials Needed:

4 weight yarn in 6 colors. 14 balls of main color, 3 balls of color A, 2 balls of color B, 3 balls of color C, 3 balls of color D, 3 balls of color E. Crochet hook in size I.

Abbreviations Used:

Chain (Ch)
Slip Stitch (Sl St)
Triple Crochet (Tr)

Cluster yarn (yarn over hook, draw up a loop in next stitch, yarn over hook and draw through first 2 loops on hooks, 3 times in same stitch. Yarn over hook and drawn through all 4 loops on the hook, ch 1 to fasten.)

Pattern:

Worked in one piece, starting at neck edge. With main color, Ch 96. Join with Sl St to form a ring.

Round 1: Ch 4, skip 1 Ch 1 Tr in next Ch space, (Ch 1, skip 1 Ch 1 Tr in next Ch space.) 9 times *Ch 2, skip 1 Ch, (Cluster, Ch 2, Cluster) in next Ch space, Ch 2, skip 1 Ch space, 1 Tr in next Ch space, (Ch 1, skip 1 Ch, 1 Tr in next Ch) 10 times. *Repeat from * to * twice. Ch 2, skip 1 Ch space, (Cluster, Ch 2, Cluster) in next Ch space, Ch 2, skip 1 Ch, Sl St in 3rd Ch at beginning of round, fasten off.

Round 2: Join in color A in any Ch 2 space after a Cluster group. Ch 4, 1 Tr in next Ch 1 space, * (Ch 1, 1 Tr) in each Ch 1 space to corner, Ch 1, 1 Tr in Ch2 space, Ch 2, (Cluster, Ch 2, Cluster) in Ch 2 space between Cluster, Ch 2, 1 Tr in Ch 2 space. *Repeat from * to * 3 times, omitting 1 Tr at end of last repeat. Sl St in 3rd Ch at beginning of round, fasten off.

Round 3: Join in color B in any Ch 2 space after a Cluster group, Ch 4, 1 Tr in same space. *(Ch 1, 1 Tr) in each Ch 1 space to corner, Ch 1, 1 Tr in Ch 2 space, (Cluster, Ch 2, Cluster) in Ch 2 space between Cluster, Ch 2, (1 Tr, Ch 1, 1

Tr) in space. *Repeat from * to * 3 times, omitting (1 Tr, 1 Ch, 1 Tr) at end of last repetition. Sl St in 3rd Ch at beginning of round, fasten off.

Repeat 2nd and 3rd rounds working in 1 round stripes of color B, main color, color C, main color, color D, main color, color E, main color, color A, main color, until work measures 22 inches. Finish with an M stripe.

For the Fringe: Wind main color around a piece of cardboard 4 inches wide and cut the yarn along one side. With wrong side facing and using 4 strands of yarn, fold yarn in half and draw loop through a Ch space at the lower edge of your poncho, pull ends through loop and tighten. Repeat in each Ch space around lower edge, working 2 knots in each 2 Ch spaces next to corners and 3 knots in corner spaces.

Simple Poncho

Advanced.

About:

This simple poncho is a beautiful piece that uses one solid color to create a stylish design. The decorative fringe pieces on the end add to the aesthetic of this pattern, making it even more enjoyable to make, and to wear. Because of the motifs used for the pattern, you will notice this pattern is more advanced in nature.

Materials Needed:

4 weight yarn. 44 balls in main color, 37 for the poncho and 7 for the fringe. Size G crochet hook.

Abbreviations Used:

Chain (Ch)
Slip Stitch (Sl St)
Triple Crochet (Tr)

Pattern:

Chain 132. Join with Sl St to form a ring.

Round 1: Ch 5, 3 Tr in same Ch as Sl St, * (Ch 2, skip 2 ch spaces, 1 Tr in each of next 3 Ch spaces) 6 times. Ch 2, skip 2 Ch spaces, (3 Tr, Ch 2, 3 Tr) in next Ch space (corner), * Repeat from * to * twice. (Ch 2, skip 2 ch spaces, 1 Tr in each of next 3 Ch spaces) 6 times, Ch 2, skip 2 ch spaces, 2 Tr in same Ch as Sl St, Sl St in 3rd Ch of 5 Ch loop.

Round 2: Sl St in Ch 2 space, Ch 5, 3 Tr in corner space, * (Ch 2, 3 Tr) in each Ch 2 space to corner space, Ch 2, (3 Tr, Ch 2, 3 Tr) in corner space. * Repeat from * to * twice. (Ch 2, 3 Tr) in each Ch 2 space to corner space. 2 Tr in corner space, Sl St in 3rd Ch of 5 Ch loop.

Repeat round 2 35 times. Fasten off.

MOTIFS (Make 48)

Chain 6, join with a Sl St to form a ring.

Round 1: (Ch 5, 1 Dc in ring) 4 times.

Round 2: Sl St in Ch 5 loop. Ch 3, (yarn over hook, draw up a loop in same Ch loop, yarn over hook and draw through 2 loops on hook) twice, yarn over hook and draw through all 3 loops on hook, Ch 2, Cluster in same Ch 5 loop, Ch 3, (Cluster, Ch 2, Cluster, Ch 3) in each Ch 5 loop, Sl St in 3rd Ch at beginning of round.

Round 3: Sl St to Ch 2 space, Sl St in space, Ch 3, 2 Tr in Ch 2 space. *Ch 2, (3 Tr, Ch 3, 3 Tr) in Ch 3 loop, Ch 2, 3 Tr in Ch 2 space. * Repeat from * to * twice. Ch 2, (3 Tr,

Ch 3, 3 Tr) in Ch 3 loop, Ch 2, Sl St in 3rd Ch at beginning of round.

Round 4: Sl St to Ch 2 space, Sl St in space, Ch 3, 2 Tr in ch 2 space. *Ch2, (3 Tr, Ch 3, 3 Tr) in Ch 3 loop, (2 Ch, 3 Tr in Ch 2 space) twice. *Repeat from * to * twice, Ch 2, (3 Tr, Ch 3, 3 Tr) in Ch 3 loop, Ch 2, 3 Tr in Ch 2 space, Ch 2, Sl St in 3rd Ch at beginning of round. Fasten off.

Chapter 2:
Home Decor

Making home decor is an excellent way to showcase your creative talents. Adorning your house with homemade curtains, doilies, or other home decor allows you to take pride in your creations and put them on display for everyone to see. These gifts also make for wonderful housewarming presents for friends or loved ones who may be moving into their new homes. Be sure to make them in a color that matches the color scheme of the room they will be displayed in!

Draped Curtains With Pom Poms

Beginner/Easy.

About:

This curtain is a simple pattern for any beginner to make. It provides an elegant, vintage look to any room it is added to. Unlike some curtains, this one should be fairly sheer, meaning it will continue to let beautiful light through, while also giving you something stunning to look at. You will certainly be proud of this project when you are done!

Materials Needed:

3 weight yarn. 38 balls of any color you desire. Crochet hook in size D.

Abbreviations Used:

Chain (Ch)
Slip Stitch (Sl St)
Double Crochet (Dc)
Triple Crochet (Tr)

Pattern:

Curtain.

Starting at the bottom of your curtain, make a chain that is about 4 yards long.

Row 1: Dc in 8th Ch from hook, *Ch 2, skip 2 Ch spaces, Dc in next Ch. * Repeat from * to * across. Ch 10 (to count as Tr, Tr and Ch 2). Turn.

Row 2: Tr, Tr (thread over 4 times) in next Dc, *Ch2, Tr, Tr in next Dc. *Repeat from * to * across, making last Tr, Tr in 3rd stitch of turning chain. Ch 5, turn.

Row 3: *Dc in next Tr, Tr, Ch 2. *Repeat from * to * across, making last Dc in 3rd stitch of turning chain. Ch 10, turn.

The last 2 rows constitute the pattern. Work in pattern until piece measures 2 ¾ yards long, or length desired.

Tie-back

Make a chain about 18 inches long. Work in curtain pattern for 5 rows, starting and ending with Dc space rows.

Ball Trimming.

Cut 2 pieces of cardboard, 1 ½ inches in diameter each. At the center of each piece, cut a ½ inch hole. Place the 2 pieces together. Cut 12 strands of thread, about 4 yards long each. Wind them around the cardboard circle until the center hole is completely filled in. Cut around the edges of the yarn, leaving the center hold still filled in.

Take a small piece of yarn and tie it around the center pieces. Remove the cardboard and trim evenly. Sew balls 6 inches apart on side and lower edges.

Cute Cubed Coaster Set With Matching Centerpiece

Beginner.

About:

This coaster set will make 6 coasters, with each coaster being approximately 5 inches squared. The matching centerpiece will be approximately 7 inches square, and works beautifully under a bouquet of flowers, or a delightful meal you are serving to your guests.

Materials Needed:

5 balls of lace weight yarn. Crochet hook size C.

Abbreviations Used:

Chain (Ch)
Slip Stitch (Sl St)
Single Crochet (Sc)
Double Crochet (Dc)

Pattern:

Doilies

(Make 6)

Ring 1: Starting at the center, Ch 10. Join with Sl St.

Round 1: Ch 1, 2 Dc in ring, (Ch 3, 3 Dc in ring) 7 times. Ch 3, Sl St to 3rd stitch of Ch 3 space. Fasten off.

Second ring: Ch 10; join. Ch 3, 2 Dc in ring, Ch 1, Sl St in corresponding Ch 3 of first ring, Ch 1, 3 Dc back into second ring. Complete as for 1st ring.

Make 8 x8 rings, joining to adjacent rings as 2nd was joined to 1st, leaving one Ch 2 loop free between joining spaces.

Edgings

Round 1: Attach thread to center Ch 3 loop of ring to the right of corner ring. *(Ch 5, Sc in 3rd Ch from hook – a pattern made) twice. Ch 1, skip 1 loop of corner ring, Sc in next loop, Ch 2, pattern, Ch 1, skip 1 loop, Sc in next loop of corner ring. (Ch 2, pattern, Ch 2, pattern, Ch 1, Sc in center loop of next ring) 6 times. * Repeat * to * around, ending with Sc in same place where thread was joined.

Round 2: Sl St to center Ch (between pattern's) of next loop, *Ch 2, pattern, Ch 2, pattern, Ch 1, Sc in next Sc, Ch 2, pattern, Ch 2, pattern, Ch 1, Sc between next 2 patterns of corner loop, Ch 2, pattern, Ch 2, patter, Ch 1, Sc in next Sc, (Ch 2, pattern, Ch 2, pattern, Ch 1, Sc in next loop between patterns) 7 times. * Repeat * to * around. Join. Fasten off.

Centerpiece

Work as for doilies but make 11 x 11 rings. Finish as for doilies. Block to 7" squared.

Striped Circle Coasters With A Scalloped Edge

Advanced.

About:

These striped circular coasters have a beautiful scalloped edge that make them look absolutely delightful. They work wonderfully as everyday coasters, or as a set that can be used during special parties, or when you have beloved guests over.

Materials Needed:

4 weight yarn, 4 balls. 2 balls of color A, 2 balls of color B. Crochet hook size H.

Abbreviations Used:

Chain (Ch)
Slip Stitch (Sl St)
Single Crochet (Sc)
Double Crochet (Dc)

Pattern:

To Make The Bottom.

Round 1: Starting at center with color A, Ch 4. 11 Dc in 4th Ch from hook. Sl St in top stitch of starting chain.

Round 2: Drop color A, attach color B, Ch 1, Sc in same place as Sl St, *2 Sc in next stitch, Sc in next stitch. * Repeat from * to * around. Join.

Round 3: Drop color B, pick up color A. Ch 3, Dc in each stitch around, increasing 12 Dc evenly around. To increase a Dc, make 2 Dc in 1 stitch.

Round 4: Drop color A, pick up color B, Ch 1. Sc in each stitch around, increasing 6 Sc evenly around.

Repeat the rounds 3 and 4 alternately until piece measures about ¼ inch larger all around than bottom of glass, ending with a round 3.

To Make The Edging.

Round 1: Drop color A and pick up color B. Turn and make Sc in back loop of each stitch around. Join.

Round 2: Drop color B, pick up color A. Sc in same place as Sl St. *Ch 5, 3 Dc where last Sc was made, skip 3 Sc, Sc in next Sc. * Repeat from * to * around. Join. Cut off color A.

Round 3: Pick up color B, *5 Sc in Ch 5 loop, Sc in next 3 Dc. * Repeat from * to * around. Join and break off.

Attach color B and, working over free loops of last Dc round of the Bottom, work a second edging as follows:

Round 1: Sc in each stitch around, increased by 8 Sc evenly around. Join.

Round 2: Same as round 2 of 1st edging, skipping 2 (instead of 3) stitches. Join and break off. Complete as for 1st edging.

Italian Table Place Mats

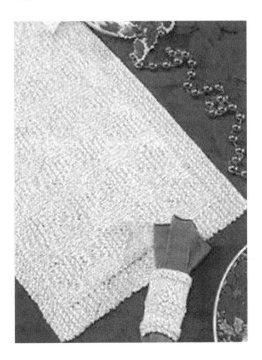

Beginner/Easy.

About:

These gorgeous place mats are a surefire way to brighten up your table. They take hardly any time to work up, and once they are designed they offer beautiful texture to an already stunning table display. Bring them out for everyday use, or use fancier colors and more delicate fibers for fancy luncheons or dinner parties!

Materials Needed:

4 weight yarn. 2 balls color A, 2 balls color B, 2 balls color C, 2 balls color D, 2 balls color E. Crochet hook in size H. 1/3 yard of natural colored linen. This is enough for 4

place mats, each of which will measure 13 ½ by 10 ½ inches.

Abbreviations Used:

Chain (Ch)
Slip Stitch (Sl St)
Single Crochet (Sc)

Pattern:

To Make The Place Mat.

Cut linen to measure 8 by 12 inches. Make a narrow hem.

Attach color A along 1 edge. Sc over hem, *Ch 1, Sc over hem. * Repeat fro * to * making Sc's about 1/8 inch apart. At corners make 3 Sc in same space, with a Ch 1 between each Sc. Ch 1 and join with Sl St to 1st stitch, Ch 1.

Row 1: *Sc over Ch 1 space, Ch 1. *Repeat from * to * around. At corners Ch 3 instead of Ch 1. Join with Sl St to 1st stitch of the row. Ch 1.

Row 2: *Sc over Ch 1 space, Ch 1. *Repeat from * to * around. At corner make 3 Sc's with a Ch 1 between each, over Ch 3 loops.

Alternate rows 2 and 3 for the entire mat, working in this pattern: 3 rows of color A, 1 row of color B, 3 rows of color C, 1 row of color B, 3 rows of color D, 1 row of color B, 3 rows of color E, 1 row of color B. The place mat will be finished with a row of color A.

Four Pointed Star Potholder

Advanced

About:

This four pointed star potholder is a beautiful crochet pattern that combines beginner level stitches with a more advanced design, to create a wonderful pattern for you to step up into if you are ready to advance beyond beginner patterns. This potholder can be used to lift hot pots out of a warm oven, or to rest them on your counter or table without wrecking your surface.

Materials Needed:

3 weight yarn, 4 balls. 2 in color A, 2 in color B. Crochet hook in size D.

Abbreviations Used:

Chain (Ch)
Slip Stitch (Sl St)
Single Crochet (Sc)

Pattern:

Use double thread therefore. Starting at center with color A, Ch 2.

Round 1: 8 Sc in 2nd Ch from hook. Join with Sl St to first Sc.

Round 2: 2 Sc in each Sc around (16 Sc). Join and cut off.

Round 3: Attach color B, Ch 1, 2 Sc in same place as thread was attached. *Sc in next 3 Sc, 3 Sc in next Sc (corner). * Repeat from * to * around, ending with Sc in same place as first 2 Sc were made. Join.

Rounds 4 and 5: Ch 1, 2 Sc in same place as Sl St. *Sc in each Sc to center Sc of next 3 Sc group, 3 Sc in next Sc. * Repeat from * to * around, ending the round as before. Drop color B.

Round 6: Attach color A and work the same as you did in round 5.

Rounds 7 and 8: Pick up color B, with B repeat round 5. Join and cut off.

Round 9: Pick up color A and repeat round 5.

Points

Row 1: Sc in each Sc across to center Sc of next 3 Sc group. Ch 1, turn.

Row 2: Work off 2 Sc as 1 Sc (1 Sc decreased.) Sc in each Sc across. Ch 1, turn.

Repeat 2nd row until all stitches are worked off. Cut off. Attach color A to center Sc of 2 Sc group and complete another point as before. Work remaining two points in same way.

Border

Round 1: Attach color B and Sc closely around, making 3 Sc at tip of each point. Join, drop color B.

Round 2: Attach color A and Sc in each Sc around, making 3 Sc in center Sc of each 3 Sc group. Join and cut off.

Round 3: Pick up color B and repeat round 2.

Comfy Oblong Pillow (Great For The Patio!)

Beginner/Easy.

About:

This simple oblong cushion is wonderful for back support, or for a small cushion to rest your head on when you are relaxing. Make it with a durable cotton so it can be safely used on the patio, without being damaged by the weather! Or, make it out of a fiber like pure wool or alpaca fiber for a designer piece for your home.

Materials Needed:

3 weight yarn. 4 balls of color A, 2 balls of color B. Crochet hook size C.

Abbreviations Used:

Chain (Ch)
Slip Stitch (Sl St)
Single Crochet (Sc)
Double Crochet (Dc)

Pattern:

Starting at narrow edge with color A, create a chain 16 inches long.

Row 1: Working with color A over a stand of color B, Sc in 2nd Ch from hook, *Working over color A with color B, Sc in next Ch. Working over color B with color A, Sc in next Ch. *Repeat from * to * across until the row measures 13 inches, ending with a Sc in color A. Ch 3, turn.

Row 2: Working over color B, skip first Sc, Dc in front loop of each Sc across. Ch 1, turn.

Row 3: Working over color B with color A, make Sc in first Dc, *Working over color A with color B, Sc in next Dc, working over color B with color A, Sc in next Dc. *Repeat from * to * across. Ch 3. Turn.

Repeat rows 2 and 3 alternately until piece measures length of your desired pillow, ending with a Sc row.

Cut off color B. With color A, Sc closely around, making 3 Sc in each corner. Join and cut off. Weave in your ends.

Chapter 3:
Blankets And Afghans

Blankets and afghans are a wonderful way to get into crocheting. With these patterns, you are generally following simple steps that are repeated throughout the entire project. On easier blankets, these steps include basic crochet stitches, while on more challenging projects they will feature complex stitches. This may sound like they are too challenging to do, however they are actually an excellent way to help advance your skills based on the fact that there is a lot of repetition. Once you understand how the pattern works, you simply repeat it for the entire project and before you know it you have mastered these new stitches! In this chapter, we will cover a variety of beginner and advanced blankets and afghans so you can begin to expand your skills while making beautiful projects at the same time.

Cozy Stripes Mile A Minute Afghan

Easy.

About:

This cozy stripes afghan is known as a "mile a minute" afghan because it is crocheted in stripes, and then those stripes are sewn together to create the entire blanket. The final product is 62 inches by 75 inches, making it a wonderfully large afghan that is excellent for snuggling up with.

Materials Needed:

Eight colors of 4 weight yarn: 17 x 1 oz skeins in color A, 17 x 1 oz skeins in color B, 17 x 1 oz skeins in color C, 11 x 1 oz skeins in color D, 11 x 1 oz skeins in color E, 11 x 1 oz skeins in color F, 9 x 1 oz skeins in color G, and 6 x 1 oz skeins in color H. Crochet hook in J.

Abbreviations Used:

Chain (Ch)
Single Crochet (Sc)
Slip Stitch (Sl St)

Pattern:

First Large Strip:

Starting at short end, with color A, Ch 9.

Row 1: Insert hook in 2nd Ch from hook and draw up a loop. Draw up a loop in each Ch stitch across, retaining all loops on hook (9 loops on hook). Draw your yarn over the hook and draw it up through 1 loop, *Draw your yarn over the hook and draw through 2 loops. * Repeat from * to * across. The loop which remains on hook always counts as the 1st stitch of next row.

Rows 2 and 3: Insert hook under 2nd vertical bar from the previous row and draw loop through. *Insert hook under next vertical bar from previous row and draw a loop through. *Repeat from * to * across, retaining all loops on hook and working to the last vertical bar. Insert hook through double vertical bar and draw a loop through (thus giving a firm edge to this side). You will have 9 loops on your hook. Draw your yarn over and draw through 1 loop. **Draw your yarn over your hook and draw through 2 loops. ** Repeat from ** to ** across.

Row 4: Make a loop in each vertical bar from the last row until there are 4 loops on hook. Draw your yarn over 3 times, insert hook in 2nd vertical bar on the 3rd row down (into the 1st row) and draw a loop through. (Draw your yarn over and draw through 2 loops) 3 times. Draw your yarn over 3 times, skip 5 bars from the same row and draw a loop through the next vertical bar. (Draw your yarn over and draw through 2 loops) 4 times. This makes a herring bone stitch. Skip the stitch directly behind the herringbone stitch that you just made and make a loop in each of next 4 vertical bars. (there will now be 9 loops on hook.) Draw your yarn over and draw through 1 loop; *Draw your yarn over and draw it up through 2 loops. *Repeat from * to * across.

Row 5: Same as 2nd row. Repeat 4th and 5th rows alternately until piece measures 72 inches long. Sl St in each vertical bar across to finish the row. Fasten off.

Make 2 more strips like this with color A, and sew one on each side of previous strip using Sl St on the wrong sides. Make 2 strips of color B and sew one to side of each previous strip as before. Make 2 strips of color C and sew to previous strips as before. These 9 stripes complete one large strip. Make 2 more large strips like this.

Second Large Strip

With color D make 1 strip. With color D make 2 strips and sew one on each side of previous strip. With color E make 2 strips and sew to sides of previous strips. Wit color F make 2 strips and sew to sides of previous strips. This completes your second large strip. Make one more large strip like this.

Sew your afghan together by alternating between the first large strip and second large strip until all of the strips have been connected. Then, make tassels and attach them to your afghan.

To make your tassels, cut ten 11-inch strands of yarn. Pull strands through center of end of stripe. Form a loop and draw ends through to form a knot. When all fringe has been made, trim it evenly. Your afghan is now done!

Rivers That Ripple Afghan

Beginner.

About:

This rippled afghan features a classic look with beautiful textured waves, and stripes in whichever colors you desire. Due to its nature, this afghan is both cozy and beautiful to look at, making it a wonderful project to spruce up any room, or to offer as a gift to a loved one. The final afghan measures 46 inches by 70 inches.

Materials Needed:

4 weight cotton yarn. 11 skeins of color A, 4 skeins of color B, and 3 skeins of color C. Crochet hook size H.

Abbreviations Used:

Chain (Ch)
Single Crochet (Sc)
Slip Stitch (Sl St)

Pattern:

With color A, Ch 245.

Row 1: Sc in 2nd Ch from hook. Sc in next18 Ch spaces. (3 Sc in next Ch spaces, Sc in next 19 Ch spaces, skip next 2 Ch spaces, Sc in next 19 Ch spaces) 5 times. 3 Sc in next Ch space, Sc in remaining 19 Ch spaces. Ch 1, turn.

Row 2: (In back loop only of each Sc throughout.) Skip first Sc. (Sc in next 19 Sc, 3 Sc in next Sc, Sc in next 19 Sc, skip next 2 Sc) 5 times. Sc in next 19 Sc, 3 Sc in next Sc, Sc in next 18 Sc, skip next Sc, Sc in last Sc. Ch 1, turn.

Row 3 to 8: Repeat 2nd row. Do not Ch 1 at end of 8th row. Drop color A, attach color C. Ch 1, turn.

Row 9: Sc in first Sc. *(Sc in Sc directly below next Sc. Long Sc made,) Skip Sc covered by the long Sc, Sc in next Sc) 9 times. Make a long Sc over next Sc, skip covered Sc, Sc in next stitch, long Sc in same place as last long Sc was made. Point made. (Skip covered Sc. Sc in next Sc, long Sc over next stitch) 9 times. Skip covered Sc, Sc in next 2 Sc. * Repeat from * to * across, ending with Sc in last Sc. Ch 1, turn.

Row 10: With color C, repeat 8th row. Cut and fasten color C. Pick up color A. Ch 1, turn.

Row 11 and 12: Repeat 2nd and 8th rows. Cut and fasten color A, attach color B. Ch 1, turn.

Row 13: With color B, repeat 9th row.

Row 14 to 18: Repeat 2nd row 4 times, then repeat 8th row once. At end of last row cut and fasten color B, attach color A. Ch 1, turn.

Row 19 and 20: Repeat 9th and 8th rows. Cut and fasten color C, pick up color A. Ch 1, turn.

Row 23 to 37: Repeat 2nd row.

Row 38: Repeat 8th row.

Repeat rows 9 through 38 5 more times, then repeat rows 9 through 30 once. Cut and fasten off. Block to measurements. Edging 1st row:

Edging

Row 1: With right side facing, using color A, Sc closely along one long edge. Turn.

Row 2: With wrong side facing, Sl St in each Sc of previous row. Cut and fasten. Work edging along opposite long edge.

Geometric Triangle Afghan

Intermediate.

About:

This geometric afghan is made by creating 108 separate blocks and then sewing them all together to create your afghan. The blanket creates a stunning design that is modern and whimsical, making it wonderful for any home or present. The final blanket is 52 inches by 70 inches.

Materials Needed:

Number 4 weight yarn. 35 balls of color A and 35 balls of color B. Afghan crochet hook size J.

Abbreviations Used:

Chain (Ch)
Single Crochet (Sc)
Slip Stitch (Sl St)

Special Stitch:

Afghan Stitch

Row 1:

Insert hook in 2nd Ch from hook and draw up a loop. Retaining all loops on hook, draw a loop up through each Ch stitch across. There should be 45 loops on your hook now. Yarn over and draw up through 1 loop. *Yarn over and draw up through 2 loops. *Repeat from * to * across until one loop remains on the hook. The one loop will count as your first stitch in your next row.

Row 2:

Insert hook under 2nd vertical bar from previous row and draw a loop through. Retain all loops on the hook as you draw a loop up through each vertical bar across. Yarn over and draw up through 1 loop. *Yarn over and draw up through 2 loops. *Repeat from * to * across until one loop remains on the hook.

Decrease:

To decrease, pass the hook behind two vertical bars on time when you are drawing loops up through your previous row. Then, finish the row as normal.

Pattern:

Block (Make 108)

With color A, Ch 36 to measure 7 ¼ inches.

Work in afghan stitch across, decreasing 1 stitch at both ends of the second row. Decrease by 1 stitch at both ends of the row in every row until three loops are remaining in the row. Yarn over and draw through all three loops. Ch 1 to fasten in your end.

Alongside the opposite end of the starting chain, attach color B and work in afghan stitch across. Decrease 1 stitch at both ends of the second row. Decrease by 1 stitch at both end of the row in every row until three loops are remaining in the row. Yarn over and draw through all three loops. Ch 1 to fasten. Cut and fasten in your end. (Create the exact same block as you made with color A.)

Sew 9 rows of 12 blocks together along the wrong side, with opposite color meeting.

Border

Round 1: Attach color B to one corner. (Sc in each Sc to next corner, 3 Sc in corner Sc.) twice. Cut and fasten off. Attach color A and work other 2 sides in the same border pattern.

Round 2 to 7: With corresponding colors, Sc in each Sc around. 3 Sc in the center of each corner Sc join with Sl St, cut and fasten ends.

Scotch Plaid Woven Afghan

Beginner.

About:

This scotch plaid woven afghan offers brilliant design without being terribly hard for anyone to create. After creating one, you will have great pride in the stunning creation you have made, and people will be surprised that you designed something so wonderful. The final afghan is 58 inches by 72 inches.

Materials Needed:

4 weight yarn. 11 skeins of color A, 19 skeins of color B, 13 skeins of color C, 3 skeins of color D. Crochet hook H. 1 Tapestry needle.

Abbreviations Used:

Chain (Ch)
Single Crochet (Sc)
Double Crochet (Dc)
Slip Stitch (Sl St)

Pattern:

With color C, Ch 219.

Row 1: Dc in the 5th stitch from the hook. *Ch 1, skip 1 stitch of Ch, Dc in next stitch. *Repeat from * to * across row. (108 meshes). Ch 4, turn.

Row 2: Dc in Dc. *Ch 1, Dc in next Dc. *Repeat from * to * across row. Ch 4, turn.

Continue rows of 1 Ch meshes, working 1 more row in color C, then cut yarn.

Attach color B and work 1 row of meses, then work 1 row in color A and 6 rows in color B. *1 row color A, 1 row color B, 3 rows color C, 1 row color B, 2 rows color A, 1 row color D, 2 rows color A, 1 row color B, 3 rows color C, 1 row color B, 1 row color A, 6 rows color B. * Repeat from * to * 4 times. Work 1 more row of color A, 1 row color B and 3 rows color C.

Weaving.

Measure a double strand of color C the length of the afghan. Allow for 10 inches of fringe at each end. Thread the yarn into the tapestry needle. Beginning at the lower right hand corner, weave in and out through the 1st row of meshes on the longest side of the blanket. Take a second double strand of color C and weave in the same row of meshes over the opposite threads.

Continue weaving twice in same meshes with one color in the following scheme: 1 in color C, 1 in color B, 1 in color A, 6 in color B. *1 mesh in color A, 1 mesh in color B, 3 meshes in color C, 1 mesh in color B, 2 meshes in color A, 1 mesh in color D, 2 meshes in color A, 1 mesh in color B, 3 meshes in color C, 1 mesh in color B, 1 mesh in color A, 6 meses in color B. *Repeat from * to * 3 times. Weave 1 mesh color A, 1 mesh color B, 3 meshes color C. Know fringe close to afghan, knot a second time ½ inch down taking half strands from one knot and half from the next knot.

Two-Tone Blocked Afghan

Beginner.

About:

This beautiful two-toned blocked afghan offers a stunning texture with a two-dimensional color. Based on the design, this afghan can easily be designed to fit into any color scheme as both a subtle yet stunning piece to adorn your room with. This pattern can also be worked up quickly if you are looking for a speedy project to work on. The final size is 51 inches by 62 inches.

Materials Needed:

4 weight yarn. 5 skeins of color A and 5 skeins of color B. (Color A and B should be a darker and lighter tone of the same color.) Crochet hook size H. Blunt end tapestry needle.

Abbreviations Used:

Chain (Ch)
Single Crochet (Sc)
Double Crochet (Dc)
Slip Stitch (Sl St)

Pattern:

One Square

Ch 20. (Ch should measure 5 inches across.)

Row 1: Dc in 4th Ch from hook. Skip 3 Ch spaces. *1 Sc in next Ch, Ch 3, 1 Dc in same Ch, skip 3 Ch. *Repeat from * to * 2 times more. 1 Sc in last Ch, Ch 3, turn.

Row 2: 1 Dc in last Sc of previous row. *1 Sc in next Sc, Ch 3, 1 Sc in same stitch. * Repeat from * to * 2 times more, ending 1 Sc in turning Ch space. Ch 3, turn.

Repeat row 2 nine times more (11 rows). Piece should now measure 4 ½ inches square. Do not cut yarn.

Ch 5, 1 Dc in same stitch, Ch 2. Working down side, space evenly (1 Dc, Ch 2) 4 times. 1 Dc in corner, Ch 2, 1 Dc in same stitch, continue around square in this manner. Cut yarn and fasten.

Make 50 Light Color and 49 Dark Color squares like the one above.

Join squares by sewing them together on the wrong side in alternating colors in rows that are 9 squares long. Sew the lengths together on the wrong side with opposite colors touching until all lengths are attached. The final afghan should be 9 squares wide and 11 squares long.

Border

Attach the darker color in one corner. Work 3 rows of Sc around the afghan, with 3 Sc in each corner to keep the border flat. Cut yarn and fasten.

Bulky Cozy Baby Blanket

Beginner.

About:

This bulky cozy baby blanket is a wonderful chunky, squishy baby blanket that makes for a wonderful gift for any baby, especially a winter baby. Be sure to use a soft baby-appropriate yarn so it is gentle against the baby's skin. The final baby blanket will measure 26 inches by 34 inches.

Materials Needed:

5 bulky weight yarn. 3 skeins of color A, one skein of color B. Crochet hook size J.

Abbreviations Used:

Chain (Ch)
Single Crochet (Sc)
Double Crochet (Dc)

Pattern:

Center

With color A, Ch 61. (About 19 inches across.)

Row 1: Yarn over hook, insert in 3rd stitch from hook, pull up a loop, yarn over hook, skip 1 stitch of Ch. Insert hook through next stitch, pull up a loop, yarn over and pull through all loops at one time. Ch 1. (The ch 1 is termed the eye of the stitch.) *Yarn over hook, insert in same space as the last stitch, pull up a loop, yarn over hook, skip 1 stitch of Ch. Insert in next stitch, pull up a loop, yarn over hook and pull through all loops at one time. Ch 1. *(Pattern.) Repeat from * to * across. Ch 1, turn.

Row 2: Yarn over hook, skip the eye of the last stitch made. Insert hook in next stitch of the same pattern space, pull up a loop, yarn over hook. Insert in eye of the next pattern space, pull up a loop, yarn over and pull up a loop through all loops at one time. Ch 1. *Yarn over hook, insert in eye of the same pattern space, pull up a loop, yarn over hook.

Insert in eye of the next pattern space, pull up a loop, yarn over and pull through all loops at one time. Ch 1. *Repeat from * to * across the row. Insert your hook in the 2nd stitch of the end Ch to complete final pattern. (29 patterns made.) Ch 1 more to turn.

Repeat the 2nd row until piece measures 25 inches. Without cutting yarn, work 80 Sc on each long side and 58 Sc on each short side. Work 3 Sc in each corner to keep project flat. Join, cut yarn, and weave in your ends.

Border

Attach color B in 1st stitch of right corner. Ch 1. Yarn over hook, insert your hook in the same space, pull up a loop, yarn over hook, insert your hook in the next stitch, pull up a loop, yarn over and pull through all loops at one time. Ch 1. *Yarn over hook, insert your hook in the same space, pull up a loop, insert hook in next stitch, pull up a loop, yarn over and pull through all loops at one time. Ch 1. *Repeat from * to * once. *Yarn over hook, insert your hook in the same place, pull up a loop, yarn over hook, skip 1 Sc, insert your hook in next Sc, pull up a loop, yarn over and pull through all loops at one time. Ch 1. *Repeat from * to * all around working the remaining 2 corners the same as 1st corner. Join with a Sl St. Ch 2, turn.

Row 2: Work in pattern same as center section, but increase 1 pattern in each corner. Join with a Sl St, cut color B, turn.

Row 3; Attach color A and work sake as last row.

Row 4: Same as previous row, but increase by 2 patterns at each corner. Cut color A, turn.

Row 5: Attach color B and work same as last row, turn.

Row 6: Same as 2nd row of border.

Row 7: Attach color A and work same as 4th row of border.

Row 8: Work in pattern increasing 1 pattern at each corner. Sl St to join. Cut color A, turn.

Row 9: Attach color B at corner, Sc in same space. *Ch 3, Dc in top of Sc just made. Skip 2 stitches, Sc in next stitches. *Repeat from * to * all around. Sl St to join, but yarn and weave in the ends.

Carriage Cover Baby Afghan

Beginner.

About:

This beautiful carriage cover baby afghan is a double-purpose piece that is wonderful for any new parent, and new baby. The afghan is heavy enough to keep a baby warm, but light enough that it can cover their carriage and keep them protected from the elements without creating too hot of an environment inside of the carriage. It's beautiful texture also makes it a fun blanket for any growing baby to explore the world through.

Materials Needed:

Fingering weight yarn. 6 balls of color C. 9 yards narrow satin. Crochet hook size F.

Abbreviations Used:

Chain (Ch)
Single Crochet (Sc)
Double Crochet (Dc)
Slip Stitch (Sl St)

Pattern:

Ch 125.

Row 1: 1 Sc in 2nd stitch from hook. 1 Sc in each remaining stitch of Ch. Ch 1 to turn each row.

Row 2: Working in back of loop of stitches only. 1 Sc in each of the next 4 Sc. *Ch 1, skip 1 Sc, 1 Sc in each of the next 4 sc. *Repeat from * to * across row.

Row 3: 1 Sc in each of the next 4 sc. *4 Dc in Ch 1, 1 Sc in each of the next 4 Sc. * Repeat * to * across row.

Row 4: Sc in each of the next 4 Sc. *Ch 1, 1 Sc in each of the next 4 Sc. * Repeat * to * across row.

Repeat last 2 rows for pattern until section measures 32 inches.

NEXT ROW: Work 1 Sc in each Sc and in each Ch 1 space.

NEXT ROW: 1 Sc in each Sc. Cut yarn and weave in the ends.

Border:

Attach yarn in any corner stitch.

Round 1: Ch 1, 3 sc in same space. Working in both loops of stitches and all around section, work 1 Sc in each Sc, 1 Sc in each row along each long side working 3 Sc in each corner stitch. Sl St to join in 1st Sc.

Round 2: (Beading) Sl St to corner stitch, Ch 3. Dc in same space. Ch 1, 2 Dc in same space. *Ch 1, skip 1 Sc, 1 Dc in each of the next 2 Sc. *Repeat from * to * to corner. 2 dc, Ch 1, 2 Dc in corner Sc and complete round to correspond. Sl St to join in 3rd stitch of Ch 3 space.

Round 3: Ch 3, 1 Dc in next stitch, 3 Dc in corner stitch, 1 Dc in each Dc and in each Ch 1 around. Work 3 Dc in each corner stitch, Sl St to join in 3rd stitch of Ch 3 space.

Round 4: (Beading) Ch 3, 1 Dc in next Dc, Ch 1, skip 1 Dc, 2 Dc, Ch 1, 2 Dc in next Dc (corner). *Ch 1, skip 1 Dc, 1 Dc in each of the next 2 Dc. *Repeat from * to * around. Work all corners to correspond. Sl St to join in 3rd stitch of Ch 3 space.

Round 5: Ch 1, Sc in same space. Work in back loop of Dc only. 1 Sc in each Dc and in each Ch 1 working 3 Sc in each corner stitch. Ch 1, Sl St to join.

NEXT 3 ROUNDS: Work in back of loop of stitches only. 1 Sc in each Sc. Work 3 Sc in each corner stitch, Sl St to join each round. Cut yarn at end of last round. Lace ribbon through beading and finish each corner with a bow.

Chapter 4:
Patterns With A Purpose

One of the best parts of crocheting is that you can design your patterns to have a wonderful purpose. For example, you can make dish cloths, toaster covers, aprons, and other such patterns that are both stylish and fun to make, while also being useful in many different ways. Once you have been crocheting for a while, being able to create something with purpose is excellent because it allows you to ensure that your craft is both enjoyable and useful. This way, you do not end up with hundreds of afghans and slippers, and no one left to give them to!

Moss Stitch Dish Cloth Pattern

Beginner.

About:

This moss stitch dish cloth pattern is excellent for creating simple dish cloths in any size you want. You can also expand the pattern so that you have tea towels by simply making it twice as long as you would for a dish cloth. They work up in just a few minutes flat, and they work wonderfully even on stubborn messes.

Materials Needed:

4 weight cotton or acrylic yarn. 1 skein in any color.
Crochet hook in size H.

Abbreviations Used:

Chain (Ch)
Single Crochet (Sc)
Double Crochet (Dc)
Slip Stitch (Sl St)

Pattern:

Ch 37. (Should be about 5.5 inches across.)

Row 1: In 2nd stitch from the hook, Dc. *Ch 1, skip 1, 1 Dc* across. Ch 2, turn.

Row 2: Dc in space made by previous Ch 1 space. *Ch 1, skip 1, 1 Dc.* Across. Ch 2, turn.

Repeat row 2 until the pattern is as long as it is wide. When you reach the end of the last row, start making your border as follows.

Row 1: Sc 3 times in the corner space. *(Ch 1, skip 1, 1 Sc) evenly across the edge. Sc 3 times in the next corner space. * Repeat from * to * until you have gone all the way around the pattern.

Row 2: Sc 3 times in corner space. *(Ch 1, skip 1, 1 Sc) evenly across the edge. Sc 3 time in the next corner space. *Repeat from * to * around. Cur off the yarn and weave in the ends.

Two-Toned Toaster Cover Pattern

Beginner.

About:

This two-toned toaster cover pattern is a beautiful project that works as a practical piece, too. You can make your toaster cover relatively quickly, and even with the most basic skills. The end result is a piece that will spruce up your kitchen with a vintage feel.

Materials Needed:

4 weight yarn. 4 skeins of color A, 2 skeins of color B. Crochet hook size H.

Abbreviations Used:

Chain (Ch)
Single Crochet (Sc)
Triple Crochet (Tr)

Pattern:

Side piece (Make 2)

Starting at lower edge with color A, Ch 80. (Should measure 11.5 inches.)

Row 1: Tr in 5th Ch from hook, Tr in each Ch across. Ch 4, turn.

Row 2: Skip first Tr, Tr in each Tr across. Ch 4, turn.

Repeat 2nd row until piece measures 4 ½ inches long.

Decrease 1 stitch at both ends of next 3 rows. (Decrease by 1 stitch by working off 2 stitches as 1 stitch.) Decrease 2 stitches at both ends of the next row. Cut off and weave in the end.

Gusset

Starting at lower edge, Ch 40. (Should measure 5 ½ inches.) Work as for side piece without decreasing until piece measures 19 ½ inches. Cur off and weave in ends.

Weaving

Row 1: (Step 1): With right side facing and a single strand of color B, weave over first Tr. *Under 2 Tr, over 2 Tr. *Repeat from * to * across. (Step 2) In same Tr row, weave under first Tr. *Over 2 Tr, under 2 Tr. *Repeat from * to * across. (Step 3) Repeat step 2. (Step 4) Repeat step 1.

Repeat first Weaving Row until all Tr rows are woven. (Be careful to keep continuity of pattern on decrease rows). With color A and right side facing, Sc around side and top edges of both side pieces. Sc across long edges of gusset.

Holding side pieces and gusset together and working through both thicknesses, Sc around side and top edges with color A. With color A Sc around lower edge. Sl St join and break off.

Frilly Edged Candy Dish

Intermediate.

About:

This frilly candy dish is a unique piece that offers a delightful texture. It looks as though a doily has been shaped into a dish which can be used to hold individual sweeties or even homemade cookies. If you want to store unwrapped candies or nuts in this dish, place a glass bowl in the center and store them in that.

Materials Needed:

Fingering weight yarn. 2 balls of any color you desire. Crochet hook size J.

Abbreviations Used:

Chain (Ch)
Single Crochet (Sc)
Double Crochet (Dc)
Slip Stitch (Sl St)

Pattern:

Ch 8. Sl St to first Ch to join.

Row 1: Work 15 Dc in ring, Sl St to join.

Row 2: Ch 5. Skip 1 Dc, Dc between next 2 Dc. *Ch 2, Dc between next 2 Dc. *Repeat from * to * around. Ch 2, Sl St to join in 3rd St of Ch 5 space. (15 meshes made.)

Row 3: Sl St into mesh space. Ch 3, 2 Dc in same space. *Ch 2, 3 Dc in next mesh space. * Repat from * to * around. Ch 2, Sl St to join.

Row 4: Ch 5. Skip 1 Dc, Dc in next Dc, *Ch 2, Dc in next Dc, Ch 2, skip 1 Dc, Dc in next Dc. *Repeat from *to * around. Ch 2, Sl St to join in 3rd stitch of Ch 5 space.

Row 5: Sl St into mesh. *Ch 5, thread over needle twice, insert needle in 1st Ch space and pull through, thread over, work off 2 loops twice, thread over needle twice, insert in same stitch, pull through, thread over, work off 2 loops twice, thread over, work off 3 loops. * Repeat * to * skip 1 mesh space, Sc in next mesh. * Ch 5, 2 Tr cluster stitches in 1st Ch, Ch 5, 2 Tr cluster stitches in 1st Ch, Skip 1 mesh space, Sc in next mesh space. *Repeat from * to * around.

Row 6: Sl St on top of petal. *Ch 5, 2 Tr cluster stitches in 1st Ch, Ch 5, 2 Tr cluster stitches in 1st Ch, Sc in top of next 2 petals. *Repeat from * to * around.

Row 7: Sl St on top of petal. *Ch 7, Sc in top between next 2 petals. *Repeat from * to * around.

Row 8: Ch 5, skip 1 stitch, 1 Dc in next Ch space. *Ch 2, skip 1 Ch, 1 Dc in next Ch. *Repeat from * to * around. Ch 2, Sl St to join in 3rd stitch of Ch 5 space. (60 meshes).

Row 9: Same as row 5.

Row 10: Same as row 6.

Row 11: Sl St to top of petal. *Ch 8, Sc in top between next 2 petals. *Repeat from * to * around.

Row 12: Ch 5, skip 2 stitches, Dc in next stitch. *Ch 2, skip 2 stitches, Dc in next stitch. *Repeat from * to * around. (3 meshes made between petals.)

Row 13: Sl St in next mesh space. Ch 3, Dc in same space. *Ch 1, 2 Dc in next mesh. * Repeat from * to * around. Ch 1, Sl St to join.

Row 14: Sl St into next Ch 1 loop. *Ch 5, 2 Tr cluster stitches in 1st Ch space. Ch 5, 2 Tr cluster stitches in 1st Ch, skip the next 2 Dc, loop, 2 Dc, loop, 2 Dc, and Sc in next loop. *Repeat from * to * around.

Row 15: Same a row 6.

Row 16: Same as row 7.

Row 17: 8 Sc in each 7 Ch loop.

Row 18: Ch 4, *1 Dc in next Sc, Ch 1. *Repeat from * to * around. Ch 1, Sl St to join in 3rd stitch of Ch 4 space.

Row 19: Sl St into Ch 1 loop. Ch 5, Dc over next Ch 1 loop. *Ch 2, Dc over next Ch 1 loop. *Repeat from * to * around, Sl St to join.

Row 20: Sl St into Ch 2 loop. *Ch 3, Sc in next loop.
*Repeat from * to * around, cut thread.

To Stiffen Your Bowl:

Boil 3 tablespoon of sugar in 4 tablespoons of water for 2
minutes. When it cool, dip the bowl into the syrup, place it
over the bottom of a pie dish and smooth it into the shape.
Fold the scalloped edges and allow the piece to dry.

Grandma's Traditional Toilet Seat Cover

Beginner.

About:

This toilet seat cover will add a touch of decor to your bathroom while also keeping your toilet free of dust. It also adds a tinge of vintage feel to your bathroom, just like grandma's house! This project is excellent for beginners, as it is easy to create though it will expand your skillset so you can take on even more complex projects in the future. Make it in any color you desire to match your bathroom decor, or as a housewarming gift for a loved one!

Materials Needed:

4 weight yarn. 4 balls in any color. Crochet hook in size I.

Abbreviations Used:

Chain (Ch)
Single Crochet (Sc)
Triple Crochet (Tr)

Slip Stitch (Sl St)

Pattern:

Starting at straight edge of center section, Ch 22.

Row 1: Sc in 2nd Ch from hook. Sc in each Ch across. Ch 1, turn.

Row 2: 2 Sc in first Sc (1 Sc increased.) Sc in each Sc to within last Sc, 2 Sc in last Sc (1 Sc increased.) Ch 1, turn.

Row 3: Sc in each Sc across. Ch 1, turn.

Repeat rows 2 and 3 alternately until piece measures 6 inches. Work without increasing for 3 more inches.

Decrease 1 Sc at both ends of the each row until 15 Sc remain. (To decrease by 1 Sc, work through 2 Sc as 1 Sc.) Cut off.

Border

Round 1: Attach yarn to first Sc of first row of center section. 3 Sc in same space. Sc closely around. 3 Sc in last Sc of first row. (End with an even number of Sc.) Sl St to join.

Round 2: Ch 1. *Sc in next Sc, Tr in next Sc. *Repeat from * to * around. Sl St to join.

Round 3: Ch 1. Sc in each stitch around. 3 sc in center Sc of each 3 Sc groups from the previous round. Sl St to Join.

Round 4: Ch 1, *Tr in next Sc, Sc in next Sc. *Repeat from * to * around. Sl St to Join.

Round 5: Repeat round 3.

Round 6: Repeat round 2.

Round 7: Repeat round 3.

Round 8: *Ch 3, skip 2 Sc, Sc in next Sc. *Repeat from * to * around. Sl St to Join and cut off. Fasten in ends.

Make a chain 54 inches long and draw through last round of loops, starting at the flat side of the toilet seat cover. Make a bow there. This will be used to tighten the cover to the seat.

Oval Bath Mat

Beginner.

About:

This simple bath mat pattern is made using cotton yarn. It is advised that you get a rubber no-slip mat to put underneath the rug to avoid accidental slips or falls. This will also help keep the mat from crumpling or folding on the floor when it is being stood on. If you make this mat to match your toilet seat cover, you will have a matching set!

Materials Needed:

4 weight cotton yarn. 6 skeins in any color. Crochet hook number H.

Abbreviations Used

Chain (Ch)
Slip Stitch (Sl St)

Pattern:

Work with two strands at once. Ch 20 (Should measure about 7 inches.) Turn.

Round 1: Insert hook in 2nd stitch from hook, draw loop out on hook. Insert hook in 3rd stitch, draw loop out on hook. Insert in 4th stitch, draw loop out on hook. Insert in 5th stitch, draw loop out on hook. (5 loops on hook.) Yarn over, draw up through all 5 loops at cone. *Ch 1, insert in single loop at back of the Ch just made. Draw loop out on hook, insert hook in outside yarn of stitch just made, and draw loop out on hook. Insert hook in stitch where complete stitch was just made, and draw loop out on hook. Insert hook in next stitch of Ch space, and draw loop out on hook. (5 loops on hook.) Yarn over, and draw up through all 5 loops. *Repeat from * to * until you reach the end of the Ch. Work along other side of foundation Ch.

Round 2: Continue with this same group of stitches for as many rounds as desired. Increases are made at the ends of the mat only. Keep work flat. Increase by making an additional group stitch in the small Ch that fastens the group stitch. As the mat grows in size, more increases as needed at the ends. Work a border of 2 or 3 rounds, using two threads of the same color.

Bumble Bee Striped Oven Mitt Pattern

Beginner.

About:

This oven mitt pattern is a simple pattern that is functional for the kitchen as well. If you stripe it between yellow and black, you get a wonderful bumble bee-like coloring which makes for a whimsical and enjoyable oven mitt. You can also choose to use whatever color stripes you prefer, or create a solid colored oven mitt. Create a pair for a complete set!

Materials Needed:

4 weight yarn in acrylic or cotton. 2 balls of yellow, 1 ball of black. Crochet hook size C. 1 bone ring.

Abbreviations Used:

Chain (Ch)
Single Crochet (Sc)
Slip Stitch (Sl St)

Pattern:

Mitt

Starting at wrist edge with yellow, Ch 21.

Row 1: Sc in 2nd Ch from hook. Sc in each Ch across. Ch 1, turn.

Rows 2, 3, and 4: Sc in each Sc across. Ch 1, turn. At end of 4th row, drop yellow.

Row 5: Attach black to first Sc. Sc in same place and in each Sc across. Ch 1, turn.

Row 6: Sc in each Sc across. Drop black. The first 6 rows establish color pattern.

Row 7, 8, 9, and 10: Pick up yellow. Sc in each Sc across. Ch 1, turn.

Row 11: Sc in each Sc across, 2 Sc in last Sc increased for thumb shaping.) Ch 1, turn.

Row 12: Repeat row 5.

Row 13: Repeat 11th row.

Row 14: Sc in each Sc across to within last 2 Sc, work off 2 Sc as 1 Sc (1 Sc decreased).

Rows 15 and 16: Repeat 13th and 14th rows. Cut off yellow and weave in the ends.

Row 17: Sc in each sc across, 2 sc in last sc. Ch 1, turn.

Thumb

Row 1: Sc in first 6 sc. Turn.

Row 2: Attach yellow to first Sc, Sc in next 4 Sc, 2 Sc in last Sc. Ch 1, turn.

Row 3: Sc in each Sc across. Ch 1, turn.

Row 4: Skip first Sc, Sc in each Sc across, 2 Sc in last Sc. Ch 1, turn.

Rows 5 and 6: Repeat 3rd and 4th rows.

Row 7: Decrease 1 sc at beginning and end of row. Cut off and weave in the ends.

Attach black at base of thumb in the same Sc as last Sc of thumb and continue to work in pattern until 23 rows have been completed.

Row 24: Sc in each Sc, decrease 1 Sc at end of row.

Rows 25, 26, 27, 28, and 29: Work in patterns without decreasing.

Row 30: Sc in each sc across, decreasing 1 sc at end of row.

Row 31: Work without decreasing.

Rows 32 and 33: Repeat last 2 rows. Now decrease 1 Sc at both ends of each row until 8 Sc remain. Cut off and weave in the ends.

Make another piece in the same way.

Holding the two pieces together with the wrong sides out and working through both thicknesses, attach black at the wrist edge. Sc closely around to other side of wrist edge. Cut off and weave in the ends. With black Sc closely around bone ring. Sew ring in place.

Chapter 5:
Advanced Patterns

Graduating from beginner's patterns to advanced patterns is a wonderful opportunity to expand your skills! When you expand from beginner's to advanced, typically the patterns themselves will continue to contain the same stitches that you are already used to, though they will use them in ways that create more advanced results. Here, I have included wonderful patterns that are sure to make you feel like an expert without having to untangle your yarn in a fuss!

Three Little Bears Amigurumi Pattern

Advanced.

About:

These three little bears are the easiest amigurumi teddys you will ever create, and they are absolutely adorable. Their ginormous ears and tiny tufts of hair are sure to capture your heart. Plus, you can play with the bears along to the three little bears nursery rhyme, making it a wonderful present for any child looking for a special present!

Materials Needed:

4 weight yarn. 9 skeins in brown, 9 yards of pink. Crochet hook size J. 24 inch square gold felt. Felt scraps in black, brown, orange, chartreuse, and white. Glue. Filling.

Abbreviations Used:

Chain (Ch)
Single Crochet (Sc)
Slip Stitch (Sl St)

Pattern:

LARGE BEAR

Body:

Ch 5, Sl St to join to form ring.

Round 1: Work 8 Sc in ring, do not join. Place a marker at beginning of each round.

Round 2: 2 Sc in each Sc.

Round 3: Work in Sc throughout, increase to 19 Sc.

Round 4: Increase to 21 Sc.

Round 5: Increase to 29 Sc.

Round 6: Increase to 35 Sc.

Round 7: Increase to 41 Sc.

Round 8: Increase to 48 Sc.

Round 9: Increase to 51 Sc.

Round 10: Increase to 54 Sc.

Round 11: Increase to 58 Sc.

Round 12: Increase to 62 Sc.

Rounds 13 to 33: Work even, cut yarn.

Dividing The Section in Half For Legs

Working through both sections at center only attach yarn in center. Work 1 Sc in 31 Sc around.

NEXT 9 ROUNDS: Work even on the 31 Sc, cut yarn. Attach yarn at center and complete 2nd leg using the same pattern.

ARMS: (Work 2). Work same as body for 3 rounds.

Round 4: Increase to 23 Sc.

Rounds 5 to 12: Work even, cut yarn.

EARS: (Work 2). Ch 10.

Row 1: Sc in 2nd stitch from hook and in each remaining stitches of the Ch.

Row 2: 1 Sc in each Sc.

Rows 3 and 4: Increase 1 stitch in 1st and last stitch.

Row 5: Work even.

Rows 6, 7 and 8: Decrease 1st and last stitch, cut yarn. Attach yarn at corner and work a row of Sc around 3 sides, cut yarn.

MEDIUM BEAR

Work 1st 8 rounds same as Body of Large Bear.

Round 9 through 31: Work even, cut yarn.

LEGS: Divide in half same as Large Bear and work across 24 Sc for each leg for 8 rounds, cut yarn.

ARMS: (Work 2). Ch 5, join.

Round 1: Work 6 Sc in ring.

Round 2: Without joining, work 2 Sc in each stitch.

Round 3: Increase to 15 Sc.

Round 4: Increase to 18 Sc.

Rounds 5, 6, 7, 8, and 9: Work even, cut yarn.

EARS: (work 2). Ch 8.

Row 1: 1 Sc in 2nd stitch from hook and in each remaining stitch of Ch. Ch 10 turn each row.

Rows 2 and 3: Work even.

Row 4: Increase 1 stitch at each end.

Row 5: Work even.

Rows 6 and 7: Dec 1 stitch at each end, cut yarn. Attach yarn at corner and work Sc around 3 sides.

SMALL BEAR

BODY: Ch 5, join.

Round 1: Work 7 Sc in ring.

Round 2: 2 Sc in each stitch.

Round 3: Increase to 17 Sc.

Round 4: Increase to 20 Sc.

Round 5: Increase to 26 Sc.

Round 6: Work even.

Round 7: Increase to 33 Sc.

Round 8: Increase to 36 Sc.

Rounds 9 through 26: Work even, cut yarn.

LEGS: (Work 2). Ch 26, join.

Round 1: Work 1 Sc in each stitch of Ch.

Rounds 2, 3, 4, 5, and 6: Without joining round, work 1 Sc in each Sc, cut yarn.

ARMS: (Work 2). Ch 5, join.

Round 1: Work 6 Sc in ring.

Round 2: 2 Sc in each Sc.

Round 3: Increase to 16 Sc.

Rounds 4, 5, 6, and 7: Work even, cut yarn.

EARS: (Work 2). Ch 6.

Row 1: 1 Sc in 2nd stitch from hook and in each remaining stitch of Ch.

Row 2: Work even.

Rows 3 and 4: Increase in 1st and last stitch.

Row 5: Decrease 1st and last Sc.

Rows 6 and 7: Repeat las row, cut yarn. Attach yarn in corner and work Sc around 3 sides.

FINISHING: Fill body sections with filler.

Use gold felt to fill the inside of your bear's ears, their feet, their hands, and their bellies. Cut eyes and eyelashes from white and black felt and place them on the bear's faces. Use pink yarn to create hair for your bears. To do this, cut the yarn into 2 inch lengths and fold them in half. Pull the fold through the top center of your bear's head and pull the ends through the fold and pull tight for the hair.

Sweetheart Toy Puppy

Advanced.

About:

This adorable puppy pattern is a wonderful pillow-like amigurumi pattern that makes for a wonderful gift for anyone of any age. It features very few details on the face, all of which can be designed using yarn, making it an excellent choice for younger children who may not do well with plastic eyes or accessories on their stuffed animals.

Materials Needed:

4 weight cotton yarn. 2 skeins color A, 1 skein color B. Crochet hook size H. Filling.

Abbreviations Used:

Chain (Ch)
Single Crochet (Sc)
Slip Stitch (Sl St)

Pattern:

PAW: With color A Ch 3.

Row 1: Sc in 2nd stitch from hook, 2 Sc in next stitch of Ch, Ch 1 to turn all rows throughout all sections.

Row 2: 1 Sc in each Sc.

Row 3: Working in Sc increase 1 Sc at beginning and end of row, cut yarn. Set aside.

BODY SECTION: With Natural Ch 3.

Row 1: 2 Sc in 2nd stitch from hook, 2 Sc in next Sc.

Row 2: Working in Sc increase 1 Sc at beginning of row.

Row 3: Increase 1 Sc at beginning and end of row.

Row 4: Repeat row 2.

Row 5: Repeat row 3.

Row 6: Repeat 3rd row.

Row 7: Increase 1 Sc at end of row.

Row 8: 1 Sc in each Sc, Ch 9. Work 1 Sc in each Sc of paw section.

Row 9: 1 Sc in each Sc and in each stitch of Ch.

Row 10: 1 Sc in each Sc.

Row 11: 1 Sc in each Sc.

Row 12: Decrease 1 Sc at end of row. (To decrease: pull up a loop in each of 2 stitches. Yarn over and work off all loops at one time).

Row 13: Decrease 1 stitch at beginning of the row.

Row 14: Decrease 1 stitch at beginning of the row.

Row 15: Increase 1 Sc at beginning of row.

Row 16: Repeat 13th row – 25 Sc.

Row 17: Repeat 12th row.

Row 18: Skip 2 stitches, 1 Sc in each of next 3 stitches. Sl St in each of next 3 Sc, 1 Sc in each remaining stitches.

Row 19: 1 Sc in each of next 14 Sc, decrease 1 stitch, Ch 1, turn.

Row 20: Increase 1 Sc at beginning of row, and decrease 1 Sc at end of row.

Row 21: 1 Sc in each stitch. Repeat last 2 rows once.

Row 22: Repeat row 20.

Row 23: Repeat row 21.

Row 25: Decrease 1 Sc at beginning of the row.

Row 26: Increase 1 Sc at end of row. Ch 3, turn.

Row 27: 3 Sc in 2nd stitch from hook. 1 Sc in next stitch of Ch and in each remaining stitch. 19 Sc.

Row 28: Increase 1 Sc at end of row.

Row 29: 1 Sc in each stitch.

Row 30: Decrease 1 Sc, 1 Sc in each of next 17 Sc, Sl St in next Sc.

Row 31: Skip Sl St, Sl St in next Sc, 1 Sc in each remaining Sc.

Row 32: Decrease 1 Sc, 1 Sc in each of the next 15 Sc, Sl St in next stitch.

Row 33: Skip 1 stitch, 1 Sc in each of next 16 Sc.

Row 34: 1 Sc in each of next 13 Sc, Sl St in each of next 2 Sc.

Row 35: Skip 1 stitch, Sl St in each of next 2 Sc, cut yarn, skip next 3 Sc, attach yarn in next Sc, 1 Sc in each of next 6 Sc, Sl St in each of next 2 Sc.

Row 36: 2 Sc in 1st stitch, 1 Sc in each of next 3 stitches, decrease in next 2 stitches. Ch 1, turn.

Row 37: 1 Sc in each stitch.

Row 38: Repeat row 36.

Row 39: Repeat row 38.

Row 40: 2 Sc in 1st Sc, 1 Sc in each of next 2 Sc. Decrease in next 2 stitches, turn.

Row 41: 1 Sc in each Sc.

Row 42: Repeat row 40.

Row 7: Repeat 2nd row.

Row 8: 1 Sc in each Sc.

Row 43: Repeat row 41.

Row 44: Repeat row 40.

Row 45: Repeat row 41. Cut yarn.

Attach yarn in 1st stitch on opposite side of the Ch between 1st paw and body section. 1 Sc in each of next 7 stitches. Sl St next stitch, cut yarn. Work another section.

EARS: (Make 2). With color B Ch 5.

Row 1: 1 Sc in 2nd stitch from hook and in each remaining stitch of Ch, Ch 1 to turn all rows.

Row 2: Working in Sc increase 1 Sc at beginning and end of row.

Row 3: 1 Sc in each Sc.

Row 4: Repeat 2nd row.

Row 5 and 6: 1 Sc in each Sc.

Row 9: Decrease 1 stitch at beginning and end of row.

Row 10: 1 Sc in each stitch. NEXT 2 ROWS:

Row 11: Repeat 9th row.

Row 12: Repeat 9th row, cut yarn.

EYES: With color B, Ch 2. 4 Sc in 2nd stitch from hook. Sl St to join, cut yarn.

NOSE: Ch 4, cut yarn leaving a length.

FINISHING: Sew 2 sections together leaving an opening for filling. Fill to desired fullness. Sew opening closed. Tack Eyes, Ears, and Nose in position. Embroider Mouth with 2 long stitches.

A Modern Crocheted Apron

Advanced.

About:

This apron pattern is a simple waistband apron that will keep your clothes clean when you are washing the dishes or working in the kitchen. It can also be used in the garden, or anywhere else that you might enjoy wearing an apron. The ruffled pockets make for a truly beautiful piece.

Materials Needed:

4 weight cotton or acrylic yarn. 14 balls of color A and 4 balls of color B. Crochet hook size H. 1 ½ yards of ribbon.

Abbreviations Used:

Chain (Ch)
Single Crochet (Sc)
Double Crochet (Dc)
Slip Stitch (Sl St)

Pattern:

WAISTBAND

With color A, Ch 15 inches long.

Row 1: Dc in 7th from hook, *Skip 3 Ch, in next Ch make Dc, Ch 3 and Dc*. Repeat from * to * across, until piece measure 12 inches long. Cut off remaining chain. Ch 1, turn.

Row 2: Make 4 Sc in each space across. Ch 3, turn.

Row 3: Skip 1st Sc, Dc in each Sc across. Ch 1, turn.

Row 4: Sc in each Dc across and in top stitch of turning chain. Cut off.

Row 5: Attach color B at beginning of last row (right side). Sc in 1st Sc. *Working over next Sc make Sc in the Dc below (long Sc.) Sc in next Sc. *Repeat from * to * across. Cut off. Work along spaces on other side of starting chain to correspond. Cut off.

Hot Springs Bedspread

Advanced.

About:

This bedspread features a delightful lacy-like texture that will add a beautiful feminine glow to your room. It will certainly press your skills into the best possible ones, and because it features repetition it is not as challenging as it may look.

Materials Needed:

4 weight yarn in cotton or wool. 36 balls of yarn in color A. 15 yards of ribbon. Crochet hook size G.

Abbreviations Used:

Chain (Ch)
Single Crochet (Sc)
Double Crochet (Dc)

Slip Stitch (Sl St)

Pattern:

Motif (Make 234.)

Ch 8, Sl St to join to form ring.

Row 1: Ch 1 and work 16 Sc into ring. Sl St to join.

Row 2: Ch 3. *Yarn over, insert in same space with joining. Work off 2 loops. *Repeat from * to * across. Yarn over and work off remaining loops at one time. *Ch 5, skip 1 Sc, cluster stitch in next stitch. (cluster stitch: yarn over, insert in stitch, work off 2 loops, yarn over, insert in same stitch, work off 2 loops, yarn over, insert in same stitch and work off 2 loops twice, then work off remaining 3 loops at one time.) *Repeat from * to * 6 times. Ch 5, Sl St to join.

Row 3: Sl St into next loop. Ch 3 and work a cluster stitch in loop. Ch 4, cluster stitch in same space. Ch 5, Dc in next loop, Ch 5. * 2 cluster stitches with Ch 4 between in next loop. Ch 5, Dc in next loop, Ch 5. *Repeat from * to * around, Sl St to join.

Row 4: Sl St into next loop, Ch 3. **Work 2 cluster stitches with Ch 4 between in 4 Ch loop. *Ch 2, skip 1 stitch of Ch, cluster stitch in next stitch. *Repeat from ** to * 4 times. Ch 2 and repeat from ** around.

Row 5: Sl St into loop. Ch 3 and **Work 2 cluster stitches with Ch 4 between in 4 Ch loop* Ch 2, cluster stitch in next Ch 2. *Repeat from ** to * 5 times. Ch 2 and repeat from ** all around, Sl St to join.

Row 6: Sl St into loop, Ch 3 and **Work 2 cluster stitches with Ch 4 between in 4 Ch loop. * Ch 4, Dc between next 2 cluster stitches. *Repeat from ** to * 6 times. Ch 4 and repeat from ** all around.

Row 7: Sl St to center of loop. Ch 1, 3 Sc over remainder of loop, 4 Sc in each of the next 8 meshes. 3 Sc in corner loop. Ch 9, turn.

Row 8: Sl St over the next Dc of previous row. *Ch 9, skip 1 Dc, Sl St over next Dc. *Repeat from * to * twice. Ch 9, Sl St in 1st Sc in corner loop. Ch 1, turn.

Row 9: *3 Sc over loop, Ch 4, Sl St in top of last Sc for picot, 5 Sc over same loop, picot 3 Sc over same loop. *Repeat from * to * in next 2 loops. 3 Sc, picot, 3 Sc in next loop. Ch 9, turn.

Row 10: Sl St between picots of next scallop, Ch 9, Sl St between picots of next scallop. Ch 1, turn.

Row 11: 3 Sc, picot, 5 Sc, picot, 3 Sc over loop, 3 Sc, picot, 3 Sc over next loop. Ch 9, turn.

Row 12: Sl St between picots of next scallop, Ch 1, turn, 3 Sc, picot, 3 Sc, picot, 3 Sc, picot, 3 Sc over loop, Sl St in last Sc of scallop below and work 2 Sc, picot, 3 Sc over remainder of each of the next 2 loops, 3 Sc, picot, 5 Sc, picot, 3 Sc over next loop, Sl St in top of last Sc in corner and work other 3 sides to correspond.

Chain Mesh Designer Gloves

Advanced.

About:

These dainty designer gloves offer warmth and style. They can be made in any size you desire, and in any color you desire, as well. They make for a beautiful dainty gift for a friend, or as an elegant addition to your own wardrobe.

Materials Needed:

Worsted weight yarn. 1 skein color A , 1 skein color B. Crochet hook size J.

Abbreviations Used:

Chain (Ch)
Single Crochet (Sc)
Double Crochet (Dc)
Slip Stitch (Sl St)

Pattern:

Forefinger, Middle Finger, Ring Finger and Little Finger

Round 1: 7 Sc in ring (do not join but continue as spiral.) Sc in Ch 1 space.

Rounds 2 and 3: Sc in each Sc.

Round 4: *Ch 3, skip Sc, Sc in next. *Repeat from * to * 3 more times. (4 Ch 3 loops made.)

Round 5: *Ch 3, Sc in next ch 3 loop. * Repeat from * to * until finger is desired length. Make fingers slightly shorter than actual finger so they fit better.

Thumb.

Ch 4, Sl St to form ring. Ch 1.

Round 1: 9 Sc in ring (do not join but continue as spiral.) Sc in Ch 1 space.

Rounds 2 and 3: Sc in each Sc.

Round 5: *Ch 3, Sc in next ch 3 loop. *Repeat from * to * until thumb is desired length.

Palm.

Lay fingers in order, and join one mesh of one finger to one mesh of other with over and over stitches. Fasten thread to outside of little finger.

Round 1: *Ch 3, Sc in next Ch 3 loop, *Repeat from * to * across palm, and continue across back of hand. Do not join, but continue as a spiral.

Round 2: *Ch 3, Sc in next Ch 3 loop, *Repeat from * to * around and around up to the thumb. Now try glove on and mark place for thumb- Sew 2 meshes of thumb to 2 meshes of glove.

Continue with pattern, working over the glove and the thumb for 6 rounds.

For the next round, decrease 1 mesh at beginning of thumb and 1 mesh after working over 3 meshes of thumb to decrease a mesh, after Ch 3 is made, Sc in next loop and then Sc in next loop). Continue is spiral as far as writs, ending at little finger side of wrist.

Cuff.

Row 1: Attach colored yarn to finishing stitch of glove. Ch 2, Dc in same Ch 3 loop. * Sc in next Ch 3 loop, Ch 2, 3 Dc in same Ch 3 loop. *Repeat from * to * to end of row. Do not join. Ch 2, turn.

Row 2: Sl St in Ch 2 loop of last shell made. Ch 2, 3 Dc in same Ch loop as Sl St was made. *Sl St in Ch 2 loop of next shell, Ch 2, 3 Dc in same Ch loop as Sl St was made. *Repeat from * to * to end of row. Ch 2, turn.

Rows 3 to 8: Same as 2nd row. After completing 8th row, cut off. Turn.

Row 9: Attach color A in last Dc made. In Ch 2 loop made at beginning of last shell, make 1 Sc, 2 Dc, 1 Sc. *In Ch 2 loop of next shell, make 1 Sc, 2 Dc, 1 Sc. *Repeat from * to * to end of row. Fasten off. Weave in ends.

Conclusion

Congratulations on completing *Easy Crocheting Patterns For Beginners!* Learning how to crochet is a wonderful way to preserve a historical craft form, while also gaining the opportunity to create incredible projects for yourself. Whether you want something decorative and whimsical or purposeful and practical, there are so many things you can do with crochet patterns.

I hope that through reading this book you were able to discover fun projects that expand your skillset while also helping you create designs that you can be proud of. Each pattern in this book was carefully chosen based on ones that would provide an excellent vintage-like feel while also being able to fit into the modern world. Plus, they were designed to ensure that no matter what your skillset is, you can confidently make many, if not all, of the patterns shared here in this very book.

Keep this book handy so you can create as many patterns as you'd like! You never know when a pattern from *Crocheting Patterns* might come in handy as a fun weekend project or a heart-felt present for a special person in your life. The more you practice making these patterns, the better your crocheting skills will become, too.

Before you go, I ask that you please take a moment to review *Easy Crocheting Patterns For Beginners* on Amazon Kindle. Your honest feedback would be greatly appreciated.

Thank you, and have fun crocheting!

Exclusive 5-day bonus course just for you!

We will be sharing top crafting mistakes to avoid, how to save money on supplies and extra craft patterns!

Simply let us know where to send the course e-mails to via this link below.

https://bit.ly/nancy-gordon

For any general feedback & enquiries, you can reach us at bookgrowthpublishing@mail.com

Printed in Great Britain
by Amazon